*ANTOINE LAVOISIER*

SARAH R. RIEDMAN

# ANTOINE LAVOISIER

## *Scientist and Citizen*

THOMAS NELSON & SONS
EDINBURGH NEW YORK TORONTO

*by Sarah R. Riedman*

ANTOINE LAVOISIER

GRASS: OUR GREATEST CROP

OUR HORMONES AND HOW THEY WORK

LET'S TAKE A TRIP TO A FISHERY

WATER FOR PEOPLE

FOOD FOR PEOPLE

WORLD THROUGH YOUR SENSES

Published in New York by Thomas Nelson & Sons and simultaneously in Toronto, Canada, by Thomas Nelson & Sons (Canada), Limited.
*Library of Congress Catalog Card Number: 57–10023*
PRINTED IN THE UNITED STATES OF AMERICA

*To Elton*

MY HUSBAND

INTELLECTUAL LEAVENER AND INDISPENSABLE HELPMATE

# *ACKNOWLEDGMENTS*

I want to acknowledge my everlasting indebtedness to all those whose laborious spadework has brought forth the riches of the past, and whose many works—listed in the bibliography of this volume—I have freely consulted in preparing my manuscript. Without their pioneering researches in two centuries of history this book could not have been written.

I am especially grateful to Denis I. Duveen, Fellow of the Royal Institute of Chemistry of Great Britain and Northern Ireland. To him go my special thanks for making available to me from his unique collection of Lavoisier materials some based on his original research on the life and work of the founder of modern chemistry; and for furnishing valuable pictures and documents not to be found elsewhere. I am particularly indebted to Dr. Duveen for his painstaking and critical reading of my manuscript, his valuable suggestions for improving it, and for his genial cordiality in giving this assistance.

S. R. R.

*February, 1957*

## *CONTENTS*

## 1. YOUNG ANTOINE

*It was* one of the days when Mlle Constance Punctis took her nephew and niece to visit the gardens of the Tuilleries Palace. They were riding in the family's coach, pulled by two horses. As the horses broke into a trot and the large iron wheels clattered against the rough cobblestones that paved the streets of Paris, they could hardly hear each other talk. Aunt Constance and little Marie sat on the cushioned seat facing the horses. Antoine sat opposite them on a smaller seat, with his back to the coachman perched outside the carriage. Antoine would rather have walked, as they sometimes did. Then he could have stopped and looked at anything that caught his attention, or he could have run ahead of his sister who clung to her aunt's hand.

At some distance from the royal gardens, the coach halted and Mlle Punctis and the children stepped out. There were no sidewalks or footpaths, and often they had to flatten themselves against the buildings when a mounted horseman or a coach thundered by.

Once inside the gardens, away from the noise and clatter of the streets, they could turn their attention to other, more interesting, things. There were the fountains, shooting differently shaped streams of water into the air, that kept the large circular pools filled. There were the pigeons to feed or to chase in all directions, as one wished.

But today Antoine was looking for the old gentleman with the curious little glass and notebook. The man was almost as old as Grandfather Lavoisier, whom Antoine still remembered. The boy liked to follow him in his strolls among the flower beds. He would stoop over a plant, look at it through the round glass, gently handle the leaf or the stem, jot a note down in his book, and then go on to the next plant or bush.

What was the old gentleman doing? He didn't mind answering the boy's questions, but Antoine couldn't understand his answers. He knew the names of some of the flowers, but the man had different names for them. Aunt Constance wasn't too helpful; she explained that the man was a botanist, hired by the King to study the plants. But what was there to study about flowers, and why did he go over the same ones day after day, and make notes in his big book?

Much later Antoine was to have a great friend who was a botanist, and he would accompany him on trips outside Paris, to identify plants. Then he would recall the sunny afternoons of his boyhood and the visits to the gardens of the Tuilleries.

Seven years before, on August 26, 1743, Antoine Laurent Lavoisier had been born into a pleasant and comfortable home. The Lavoisiers' house stood in a garden on a dead-end street in a quiet and fashionable part of Paris. For most French people those were times of poverty and misery, trouble and war. But in the sheltered home of his well-to-do parents, none of these touched Antoine. The Lavoisiers were originally farmers, but they had been prominent lawyers for several generations. Antoine's father, Jean Antoine, was attorney to the Parlement of Paris, the chief judiciary court of France. His mother came from a prosperous family; her father, too, was a lawyer and secretary to a Vice-Admiral of France.

According to Roman Catholic custom, the baby boy was baptized on the day of his birth in the nearby parish church of St.-Merry. His parents did not have to search for a name to give him. He was their first-born and a boy. According to family tradition, the Lavoisiers for some two hundred years had always named their eldest sons Antoine, and so the baby was christened.

When Antoine was two years old, his sister was born. The two small children had a happy life. Antoine and little Marie had to walk only a short distance to the banks of the nearby river, the Seine, to watch the barges loaded with cargo from Le Havre and Rouen. They strolled in the beautiful Tuilleries gardens which surrounded the King's palace. They even visited the palace itself and saw the palace guards in their colorful uniforms. In the summer-time, they went to the old Lavoisier home in the country, at Villers-Cotterets, for their vacation. There they could romp in the fields and wander in the forest.

Then suddenly everything changed. When Antoine was five, his mother died. Monsieur Lavoisier and the children said good-by to their happy home and moved in with Madame Punctis, Antoine's grandmother.

Madame Punctis had recently been widowed. She lived with her younger daughter in a lovely old house. This new home, too, was a happy one. Antoine and Marie could still walk or ride to the river and visit the great palaces. But the best thing about living with Grandmother was Aunt Constance. She was only twenty-two and she devoted herself completely to the two motherless children who adored her. She took a maternal pride in all of Antoine's achievements and rejoiced in his successes. When in later years he was away from home on a long trip, they wrote each other frequent and affectionate letters.

Antoine's father never married again, though he was still young when his wife died. Father and son were very close friends throughout their lives. Jean Antoine found in his son a satisfying companion, and Antoine looked to his father for a friendship he never found elsewhere.

Antoine did not go to school until he was almost eleven; until then he was probably tutored at home. His father was ambitious for him and wanted to give him the best possible education. He chose for him his own old school, the College of the Four Nations, or Collège Mazarin, which had been founded by Cardinal Mazarin more than a century earlier. It had been planned originally as a boarding school for thirty young noblemen from four provinces which had been reunited to France by a treaty in the seventeenth century. The building is still standing; today it houses the

Academy of Sciences of which Lavoisier was to become a famous member.

Mazarin College was considered the best school in Paris and also the most expensive, but Antoine's father and his wealthy grandmother paid the high fees willingly. The boy entered as a day student. Every morning, except Sunday, he crossed the Seine by the famous bridge, *le Pont-Neuf*, near the Cathedral of Notre Dame, to attend his classes.

The scholar soon showed himself to be worthy of the school. Antoine not only learned well and quickly from his teachers but also began to make his own observations. He would jot them down in a notebook, think about them, and draw his own conclusions. He seemed to thrive on hard mental work. Soon he won a prize for diligence, another for an impromptu speech, and still others in composition and the classics.

Among the essays he submitted to his teachers was one on whether the desire to record one's name and work in history was human and reasonable, and one on the necessity for accuracy in the search for the truth. The subjects of these two essays were strangely symbolic of the goals Lavoisier was to seek. All his life he sought both fame and scientific accuracy. He spoke and wrote well. In fact, at first he wanted to become an author. He planned a play, "The New Héloise," and even wrote a few scenes for it.

When he was seventeen, Antoine won the second prize for rhetoric in the annual competition for all schools in France. But tragedy touched his life that same year. His sister died at the age of fifteen. All of the family's hopes now rested on Antoine.

His literary ambitions did not last long. Unlike most schools of that day, the Collège Mazarin offered its students lectures in science, and young Lavoisier showed his enthusiasm for the subject. Fortunately he had exceptional teachers, among them outstanding scientists. They encouraged the brilliant student to make original investigations.

The man who taught him astronomy and mathematics was Abbé Nicolas Louis de Lacaille. As head of an expedition to the Cape of Good Hope, organized by the Paris Academy of Sciences in 1750, this eminent astronomer had directed the work which led to calculating the circumference of the earth. During the course of the four-year expedition, many new stars had also been noted and charted.

Antoine was less fortunate in his chemistry teacher. Professor Bourdelin, the King's physician, was of the "old school." His high professional standing did not permit him to engage in the "menial" work of experimenting. Heating crucibles over charcoal-burning furnaces was messy work and soiled one's hands and clothing. So the professor delivered dull lectures. His bored listeners waited impatiently for what was to come next—the demonstration.

According to custom, the professor's lecture was followed by experiments by a demonstrator. The science sessions were given in the theater of the Jardin du Roi. The students and distinguished visitors occupied tiers of seats arranged in a semicircle. The lecturer's table, placed at a lower level, was in full view of the audience. The demonstrator's experiments attracted not only students but also mature scientists, authors, philosophers, and even ladies and gentlemen of the Court, the elite of the Parisian intellectuals. Among the notables at these demonstrations,

Lavoisier more than once saw the philosopher and editor of the famous *Encyclopédie,* Denis Diderot. Lavoisier considered himself fortunate when, on one occasion, he borrowed Diderot's notes on the lectures, studied them, and made his own comments on the chemical elements.

As Professor Bourdelin's lectures came to an end, he would say, "Such, gentlemen, are the principles and the theory of this operation, as the demonstrator will now prove to you by his experiments." At that point the long-awaited demonstrator would take up where the professor had left off. But sometimes his experiments proved just the opposite of the "theory" the professor had presented.

The demonstrator in chemistry was Guillaume François Rouelle, known throughout Europe for his clear presentation of chemical facts. Rouelle threw himself heart and soul into his demonstrations. One student described him this way: "He usually arrived at the lecture room elegantly attired in a velvet coat, wearing a well-powdered wig, and with a little hat under his arm. Calm enough at the beginning of his lesson, he gradually warmed up to it. If his train of thought became obscure, he was impatient; he would put his hat on a piece of apparatus, take off his wig, take off his cravat, then, talking all the time, he would unbutton his coat and waistcoat and discard them, one after the other. After his ideas became clear, he was animated, he let himself go, trusting to his inspiration, and his illuminating experiments entranced his audience."

It is easy to understand why Rouelle did so much to popularize science in eighteenth-century France. For Lavoisier he did more than that. Rouelle was a great teacher and he directed and inspired many young chemists of his day. Where science was concerned, he had no use for empty words and obscure phrases. Science, he taught, thrives on experiment, not speculation. The Latin inscription prominently displayed in his laboratory was a constant reminder to his students that facts must be checked by experiment; translated it said, "Nothing is in the mind which is not first experienced by the senses."

It was Rouelle who taught Lavoisier the methods of science—to verify facts by experiment, to search for new ideas from the facts. These teachings bore fruit in the fertile mind of his logical and industrious pupil. Antoine never forgot these precepts in probing the mysteries of chemistry.

Of all Antoine's teachers, Rouelle probably influenced him the most, but another instructor became his colleague and friend. This was Jean Étienne Guettard, his teacher in mineralogy and geology. Guettard was one of the founders of the science of geology and a pioneer in making geological maps. While he was still at college, Lavoisier went on many excursions with Guettard. Later he joined him on a lengthy trip to make a geological survey for the government.

Botany and anatomy, chemistry and mathematics, meteorology and geology—Lavoisier was interested in them all. His books were filled with notes on chemical elements. With his botany professor, Bernard de Jussieu, he went to the palace garden at Versailles to identify plants and arrange them according to the new scientific classification of Linnaeus. At home, he set up a barometer so he could study the facts about weather. Work, work, work! So many things to investigate, so many questions to answer. He simply did not *want* to do anything else.

Then, when he was seventeen, the moment came when

Antoine had to choose a profession. He had been graduated from Mazarin College. What next? Of course his father was a lawyer, and the law was the traditional profession on both sides of his family. And so for the next three years young Lavoisier was a student at the School of Law. But every minute he could spare from his legal studies was spent on mathematics, geology, astronomy, biology, and chemistry. He could not keep away from science.

While he was a law student, Antoine would sometimes pretend he was sick so that he would not have to attend social functions. For several months he lived only on milk. He grew so pale that he convinced his friends he really *was* ill. One of them sent him some cereal with a note: "Your health, my dear mathematician, is like that of all literary men, whose minds are stronger than their bodies; so spare your studies and believe that a year longer on earth is worth more than a century in the memory of men."

In 1763, at the age of twenty, Antoine was graduated from the School of Law. He had a good education in the classics and literature. He could write in a clear, logical style. He had studied experimental science under some of the best teachers of France. This was a liberal education for anyone. For a young man like Antoine, with a brilliant, searching mind and a zest for study, it was the preparation for a great career in science.

But Lavoisier was not only a theoretical scientist. During his lifetime many important events were to take place in France. Because of his varied talents and interests, Lavoisier was destined to play a great part in the affairs of his country.

## 2. FRANCE IN THE MID-EIGHTEENTH CENTURY

*After the death* of Louis XIV, France was for a while ruled by a regent, Philip of Orleans, whose duty it was to protect and act for the new King, Louis XV, the great-grandson of the old Louis. For a few short years after he came to the throne in 1715, this sickly boy was called "the well-beloved," but before long he was known as "the well-detested." By 1750, the year of the Paris riots, he dared not show his face on the streets. Madame Pompadour, the lady who ruled his Court, was equally hated because of her cruelty and extravagance. As they marched in crowds through the streets of Paris, the rioters shouted: "Shave the King for a monk! Hang Pompadour!"

At this time Antoine was seven years old. In the house on the Cul-de-Sac Pecquet, bordering on the gardens of the convent of the Brothers of Mercy, and later in his grandmother's beautiful home, life was pleasant and peaceful. Within the warm family circle Antoine knew only loving care and the admiration of his proud relatives. Even the walks he took with his father or his aunt were mostly within the gardens of their pleasant neighborhood on the right bank of the Seine River.

But sometimes they returned home by way of the narrow alleys of the city's slums where young Antoine caught his first glimpses of the wretched life of the people to whom the splendors of Paris were only a painful reminder of their miserable poverty. The children of these crowded, dirty streets had no love for the well-dressed and well-fed sons of the wealthy. Antoine clutched his father's hand, fearing the scoffing urchins and hungry people who eyed him suspiciously. He would always love the city of his birth, which he was rarely to leave; but though he lived in comfort, he would never completely forget that many of the people of France knew misery and want.

What Antoine did not see of Paris, he heard discussed in his grandmother's drawing room. There the guests talked about the vices of the King, the wicked extravagances of Madame Pompadour, the burdensome taxes, and the sorry state of the Royal Treasury.

The boy listened to tales of the recent eight-day riots, when the barefoot, ragged Parisians, despite the bitter cold, had taken to the streets to demonstrate against the police. The King had offered a bonus for every homeless child picked up and sent off to work in the French colonies in America. So his police were snatching children from the streets, to be shipped to faraway Louisiana plantations.

Orphaned or not, no child was safe alone outside his house.

Nor was there trouble only in Paris. Beneath the surface, all of France was seething. In Toulouse, there were food riots, and in Rouen the peasants broke into granaries, took the grain, and sold it at prices they thought just. Louis XV had spoken the truth when he said, *Après moi, le déluge* ("After me, the flood"). In his own lifetime, Antoine was to see the flood rise to sweep away the evils of the old regime of France.

What was eighteenth-century France like, to make its people boil with anger? Antoine was not to find the answer to this question in his school books nor in his classes at the Collège Mazarin. But he had already learned that France was both rich and poor, thriving and wretched, powerful and weak, enlightened and superstitious, growing and decaying. People talked about it in the salons, as the gatherings in the drawing rooms of intellectual ladies were called; actors spoke of it in the theaters, and wits satirized it in the press. Poets wrote of it in verses and politicians in pamphlets.

There were almost 25,000,000 people living in France, and they all belonged to one of three social groups or estates. Clergymen—130,000 bishops, abbots, and priests—made up the First Estate; 100,000 titled nobles, most of them members of the King's Court, constituted the Second Estate. All the other people were the Third Estate.

By far the largest part of the Third Estate were the 22,000,000 peasants, but it also included the workingmen of the cities, the laborers on the roads, the artisans, shopkeepers, innkeepers, stock farmers, blacksmiths, and coachmen, as well as the bankers, merchants, lawyers, judges, doctors, scientists, dramatists, and philosophers. The majority were poor, but there were those, like the financiers, merchants, and professional men, who were prosperous, and even very rich. It may seem strange that the poor peasants, the wealthy merchants, and the learned professional people, all with different needs, could find a common ground on which to oppose the other two estates. But they did, and there were good reasons for it.

The Lavoisier family, neither titled nor otherwise royally privileged, belonged to the Third Estate, and were part of the professional group from which came many leaders of the French Revolution.

The sharp lines dividing the French people into three groups had been drawn many centuries before Antoine was born. The Estates were part of a very old way of life—feudalism—that had prevailed in France and most European countries during the Middle Ages. At that time most of the people lived outside the towns. They were known as serfs, and they worked the land owned by the nobles. From the land they got not only their food but almost everything they used. The nobles also received revenues from the land—produce—in return for which they pledged military protection to the serfs in the almost constant wars. Some of their income the landowners gave to the King, and from their ranks came the soldiers to fight his wars. For these services the nobles were exempted from paying taxes in cash into the King's treasury; actually, they had little money to contribute anyway.

The clergy made their contribution to the King in the form of prayers and blessings, in return for which they, too, were exempt from taxation. They also were permitted to take a share of the produce of their land which was worked, like that of the nobles, by the peasants.

The burghers, or citizens of the towns, were the only ones who paid their taxes in money. Indeed, they were glad to do so, for not only did they have the money to pay, but by these payments they were exempted from military service. In addition, they tried in this way to buy the King's approval of a uniform currency, civil law courts, and other benefits to their commerce.

This old form of society worked well as long as most of the people were attached to the land and most of the country's wealth was in the hands of those who owned the land. The division into classes had grown out of the way the people had made their living. But by the eighteenth century social and economic changes were taking place, and the three-class system, no longer suited to the new way of life that was developing, came to be known later as the *ancien régime,* or "old system."

Many peasants were acquiring their own land, and even more feudal aristocrats were losing theirs by selling them to rich members of the Third Estate. Numbering only about 100,000, the nobles owned one-fifth of all the land in France, and by title were still the heads of their peasants (formerly serfs). But the nobles had ceased to be feudal *seigneurs,* or lords. Their former feudal power now was in the hands of a central authority, the King, who had his own army.

No longer comprising the military defense of the peasants, the nobles served no useful social purpose; nevertheless, they still collected heavy taxes as landowners. As members of the King's Court they enjoyed special privileges, including tax exemption, and in return they graced the Court, advised, amused, and even dressed the King. They arranged hunts, supervised the royal hunting grounds, and planned the lavish parties for which the French rulers were famous. The nobles had become a parasitic class whose only functions were to collect unjust taxes and dance attendance upon the King and his Court.

The clergy owned another fifth of the land (the best of which belonged to the bishoprics, abbeys, and convents), and were supported by the income from these church properties. All French peasants paid church taxes called tithes, but the clergy—like the nobles—and their properties were exempt from all royal taxes; they were required only to make a present, once a year, to the King.

Not all clergymen, however, were wealthy. The parish priests, who ministered to the poor, taught their children, and took care of the sick, lived the lives of the people and were themselves poor, the income from their meager church lands going to support the bishops. And it was only the bishops and abbots, wealthy and influential, who were part of the King's Court.

The Third Estate, which included the financiers and merchants, was now emerging as the most powerful group. Industry and commerce had already begun to flourish under the earlier King, Louis XIV, and now new towns were springing up and the population of older ones was growing rapidly. The artisans, who had worked for themselves and had been protected by organizations called guilds, now had to compete with laborers moving to towns from the country; these craftsmen had to hire themselves out for wages to the owners of increasingly large manufacturing establishments. The owners of the workshops, as well as many other townsmen, became more and more wealthy.

But the rapid growth of the Third Estate was being hindered by the old feudal system. Its members were heavily taxed to support the clergy, the idle nobles, and a dissolute king, and the taxes became more and more burdensome. Merchants sending goods from one province to another had to pay customs duties at each border, as well as town fees on all goods brought to market. Trade was hampered at every possible point, to increase the revenues of the royal treasury. There were land taxes, poll taxes, taxes on salt and tobacco, tithes, customs—but still the King's treasury was always depleted.

The peasants' lot was the worst of all. Though there were some who were fairly well-to-do and owned land, the majority owned no property. They were tenant farmers, laborers, or servants (some were still serfs), permanently bound to land they could never own under this system. They worked for the landowner, and some still grazed their livestock on common pastures. They had to build roads, canals, and castles for the overlord who prevented them from selling their wheat or wine before he had sold his, and forbade them to harvest their share of the crops before they had first filled his granaries and storerooms. The peasants could take their grain only to the manor mill, to which they paid a fee; they had to pay another fee for using the manor wine press, and still another to the manor bakery in which they were forced to bake their bread.

The royal hunting grounds and all game were sacred. Royal decrees forbade the building of fences to keep out the hares, deer, and wild boars that trampled down the fields, and the peasants were not allowed to destroy them, even though they ruined the crops. Then there were the perpetual dues to the landowner, paid in both cash and produce, plus a tenth of the main crops paid to the church, and the *taille*, or property tax, the *vingtièmes* (income tax), the *gabelle* (salt tax), and the *capitation* (poll tax), all paid to the King. Under the burden of these taxes, the peasants lived little better than their cattle and often went hungry. They slept on straw and wore rags, and they and their children died in epidemics of smallpox and typhus.

Nor were the workers in the cities much better off than the peasants. Their working day was sixteen hours long, from four o'clock in the morning until eight at night. A mason earned 2.3 francs a day, a weaver 75 centimes, a miner 1 franc, a woman spinner 30 centimes. In Paris, 1 franc and 10 centimes bought about two pounds of meat or butter, but since it took a whole day's pay to buy six pounds of bread, there was rarely either meat or butter on the workers' tables.

It was the children of these city workers whom Antoine saw when he walked with his aunt or his father, and who looked at him with envy and suspicion. No doubt this troubled him, but he was a normal boy with his studies and his playmates to occupy his time and attention. He might not have been deeply impressed had his family elders and their friends not spoken seriously and often about the plight of the country; in later years Antoine remembered their conversations. Because of them, much of what he did as a mature French citizen, trained as a scientist, was related to and guided by the needs of his countrymen.

# 3. THE PATH OF A SCIENTIST

T*o please* his father and to continue in the tradition of his family, Antoine studied law. But he still found time to attend science lectures, and when he was graduated as a lawyer, he was also as well prepared to undertake research work as any young scientist of his generation.

True, the science curriculum was no great challenge, even to students with less ability than Lavoisier had. The reason for this was simple: there just *wasn't* much science at that time. A beginning high school student today has to learn more chemistry than was known by anyone then. Chemistry teachers taught only what had been handed down for centuries from the great Greek thinkers, based on the principle that all substances are formed from different combinations of four "elements"—earth, air, fire, and water. It was not yet known that water is a chemical compound of *two elements,* that air is a mixture of gases, *two* of which are *elements,* that earth is made up of *many compounds* containing *several dozen elements,* or that fire is not even a substance, let alone an element.

This may be hard to believe—but it wasn't then. For instance, if you boil water for a long time, a small amount of earthy matter or sediment is left after evaporation. Observing this, but not having our present knowledge, chemistry students of 190 years ago wrote in their notebooks that water is at least partly changed into earth.

Reasoning from their experiments, they thought that other substances could also be changed into something quite different. For example, when they dipped a steel file into a copper sulphate solution, which is deep blue, the file became coated with a film of copper and the blue color disappeared. Antoine and his fellow pupils must have been as fascinated by this process of copper plating as we are today. But we know that the solution was not "changed into" copper—as they thought—because we know the copper was there all the time, chemically bound up with the suphate salt. Even more intriguing was the idea, believed for hundreds of years, that lead could be changed into silver, because after heating the lead a long time the experimenters found a small amount of silver in the crucible.

The facts are the same today as when Antoine went to school; only the explanation differs. The earthy matter actually is the residue left after the purified water evaporates and forms steam; the copper sulphate salt breaks up chemically into its two parts; the lead ore is impure lead, containing some silver. Lavoisier's teachers explained all three processes as examples of *transmutation*, or the changing of one "element" into another—water into earth, iron into copper, lead into silver. And the forefathers of the modern chemists, the *alchemists* as they were called, were sure that someday they could change lead into gold.

For lack of a better explanation, the four-element idea persisted, though from time to time it was questioned. An Englishman, Robert Boyle, the author of a little book called *The Sceptical Chymist* (1661), had argued against it from these well-known facts: When wood is burned in an open fire it forms ashes and soot (two products); if heated by "distillation" in a *closed* vessel it yields charcoal, oil, vinegar (acetic acid), spirit (volatile liquid), and water (five products). How then can there be only four elements, always the same? Fire, he said, does not release *elements*, but only rearranges the many particles in the substances into new *compounds*. He went further, and defined an element in these words:

> "I mean by Elements, . . . . certain Primitive and Simple, or perfectly unmingled bodies; . . . . Ingredients of which all those call'd perfectly mixt Bodies are immediately compounded. . . ."

Almost a century later this definition was all but forgotten. The compositions of water and air were not known; the rusting of iron was not understood, while burning was supposed to remove a mysterious "element of fire" called *phlogiston*.

The science of chemistry was not even born when Antoine was about ready to leave the Collège Mazarin and begin his researches. He was to be a pioneer, a founder of the new science, chemistry. But building a science meant that a lot of old and cherished traditions and ideas had to be removed. In the laboratory and in the forums of learned men Lavoisier, as one of the builders, was to meet with violent opposition in the struggle between the new chemistry and the remnants of ancient alchemy. But first he had to go through the training required of a soldier of science.

For Lavoisier, this training was anything but a tedious routine. It was part of his existence, as satisfying as a hobby and as consuming as one's lifework. While still a schoolboy, he had become interested in weather forecasting. He thought that if enough information were gathered about the motion of the air layer, it would be possible to discover laws of weather. So a barometer was set up in his home in the Rue du Four-St.-Eustache, and several times a day, with the utmost regularity, he recorded the readings. Whenever he was away from home, the rest of his family took over this daily chore. For thirty years the record was never interrupted.

On holidays and summer vacations at the family's country estate, he spent his time wandering in the forest, studying the plants underfoot, the rocks, the fossil remains, and the living creatures of the woods. And always, notebook in hand, he carefully recorded what he saw. It is not surprising that the eager pupil should have attracted the special attention of his teachers. Among them was the well-known geologist Jean Étienne Guettard who became a friend of Lavoisier and his family. Together they made countless excursions into the country around Paris, collected and classified specimens, and later undertook an official geological project.

Some of Lavoisier's work was of immediate practical benefit to his countrymen. In 1765, the Academy of Sciences offered a prize for an essay on lighting the streets of Paris (even large towns at that time were lighted only with candles or oil lamps). For weeks, using what he knew of physics, Antoine studied the different kinds of lamps and fuel, even making a darkroom in his home with black curtains. When his eyes were sensitized by the complete darkness, he was able to detect very small differences in lighting power.

The problem was how to get the best lighting with the least expense. What was the best fuel, what kind of wick would best spread the light, and what shape of reflector would bring the most light to the city? Lavoisier's essay did not win the prize but in recognition of its excellence the King awarded a gold medal to the young scientist.

Professor Guettard was an old man when the government chose him to prepare a geological map of France. This meant long, tiring, and even dangerous trips into untraveled parts of the country, miles from Paris. Was there anyone better prepared than his favorite student to share in this work?

One evening in June 1767, Guettard visited the Lavoisiers. Antoine's father had by now given up the idea of his son's ever becoming a professional lawyer. It was clear to him, if somewhat disappointing, that Antoine, now a prize winner in science, was going to follow the path of a scientist. So he made no attempt to stand in his son's way when Guettard proposed that Antoine join him on his tour of Alsace-Lorraine, in northeastern France.

Together they worked out elaborate plans and bought

thermometers, barometers, hydrometers (to measure the density of water), and all sorts of other instruments. At least there were no train schedules to be worked out. In those days people traveled mainly by horse-drawn coach or carriage, but where the scientists were going, roads were either not yet built or so poor that a coach would be useless; they must, therefore, travel on horseback.

Aunt Constance was both excited and depressed at the thought of her nephew's long and dangerous journey. Her mother had just died, leaving her in complete charge of her beloved Antoine. He was now almost twenty-three, and with his grandmother's legacy (released to him by M. Lavoisier before the legal age of twenty-five) he was financially independent. But to Mlle Punctis, Antoine was still only a boy. She was proud of the opportunity offered him, but the prospect of his leaving made her sad and anxious for his safety. Now and then she would enter into the conversation, trying to include in the plans the clothes he would need, little things to make him comfortable, how they would keep in touch while he was away.

At last everything was ready, and one afternoon, on horseback, teacher and student finally set out on their scientific expedition.

During part of their journey they had an artist with them, to paint panoramic views, and a water color preserved from that time shows us a landscape with a pedestrian and four men on horseback in the foreground. The pedestrian, who wears peasant clothes and a large Alsatian hat, was evidently a local guide. Three of the horsemen undoubtedly are Guettard, Antoine, and Joseph, a household servant of the Lavoisier family. The fourth mounted figure, some distance behind them, is the artist himself, attempting to catch up with the others at a gallop; he carries a supply of artists' paper on his back and is apparently trying to rejoin his companions after falling behind while sketching.

Though armed against robbers, and accompanied by friends and a servant, still Antoine's feelings were mixed. It was his first trip away from his family, and the mountains of Vosges seemed distant and strange; yet there was nothing he wanted more than what he was sure to gain from this experience.

His first letter was to his aunt. It was written from Brie-Comte-Robert where the travelers stopped at the end of their first day:

June 15, 1767

"Mademoiselle and very dear Aunt:

"We arrived yesterday at seven-thirty in the evening; the horses and men in good condition. We are going to start out in a quarter of an hour. We are happy and well. The horses appear fit and have good appetites. So there's good reason to hope that all will go well. We will sleep at the Red Inn tonight. I have the honor to express my sentiments of high regard and tenderness.

"At five-thirty in the morning.

"M. Guettard sends you his best wishes, and asks you please to send the enclosed note to Mlle Marianne [his housekeeper], if she is still in Paris. . . . If not, he plans to write from Troyes.

"Best wishes to everyone at home."

From Troyes Antoine wrote to his father:

June 18, 1767
6 A.M.

"Monsieur and very dear Father:

"We arrived here yesterday at midday. We have seen Abbé de Chavigny who entertained us royally and took us to visit the places of interest. We are leaving soon to join him for breakfast. . . . The horses have stood up very well in spite of the long trip. . . . If you receive my letter in time, please send me, at Bourbonne, a package of weights which you can pick up from M. Chemin; they should weigh close to a quarter-grain. I need them for the hydrometer; it is inconvenient to buy them in every village. . . . This letter is intended for both you and my aunt. I will write again from Chaumont or from Lancques."

On June 18th, Mlle Punctis wrote to Antoine:

"I can't tell you, my dear, how much satisfaction your letter gave us, in letting us know you and your companions are in good health. We were impatient to have news of the beginning of your journey which seems to have been a happy one. God grant that your prudence will sustain you and that the risks you take will be well repaid. I can't tell you how much your going has concerned your father. . . . Be assured that I live only to make you happy. . . . Best wishes to Joseph from myself and the rest of the household."

He wrote to his aunt on June 20th, as follows:

> "It's scarcely eight days since I left Paris, but it seems to me as though it has been months. I can't tell you how often I think of you and my dear father and everyone else. . . . M. Guettard's cheerfulness makes our trip a most agreeable one."

A letter from both his aunt and his father on June 21st reads:

> "Here, my dear boy, are the weights you wanted. I hope you will receive them at Bourbonne. They are not as good as yours, but M. Chemin says they will do. You will undoubtedly make good use of them, and I'm happy to be able to serve you usefully."

Many such exchanges followed over the months. Aunt Constance continued to express her anxiety about his safety, while Antoine did his best to reassure the family with letters as often as he could reach the horse-drawn mail coach.

He also kept a diary in which he described the slope of the land, the types of soil, and the kinds of vegetation he found; he recorded the temperatures and densities of river and mineral waters, and described the workings of mines and quarries. Climbing to the highest point of the Vosges mountains, he collected specimens of all kinds, for himself as well as for the expedition.

One letter, probably to M. Bertin, a government official, was posted on July 25th from the village of Lancques. In it Antoine describes the iron mines in Bassigny, the principal resource of that province:

> "We have still to survey part of the mines, and we hope to be able to complete the collection on our return.
>
> "We will begin tomorrow to enter a more varied countryside. We're going to the mineral waters of Bourbonne. . . . M. Guettard will send you specimens of different things he will find there.
>
> "The objects in the following detailed list have been shipped from Chaumont to Bassigny. They are in two different boxes."

Among the items listed are:

> "Flat calcareous stones from the first layer of the ledge of D'Orsay, on the road to Nainvilles near the Forest of Crete.
>
> "A piece of forged iron from the forge of Lancques, taken from the mine.
>
> "Iron ore from rock composed of small, blackish sand, held together by a yellow earth. . . . It yields a very good iron.
>
> "Limestone which contains rhomboid crystals of a semitransparent spar."

Near the end of the journey, we learn that young Lavoisier bought a number of books from Amand Koenig in Strasbourg. On October 6th, when he was already on his way home, the bookseller wrote to him in Paris:

> "I have sent the books which I believe should reach Paris about the 24th of this month. You will find them with those of M. Guettard, in a large box, well packed and marked: weight 288 pounds. I have arranged for the cheapest possible transportation charge. I hope the books will arrive in good condition. . . . Here is your bill which amounts to 533 livres, 5 sous. I flatter myself that you will be satisfied that my estimate of approximately 500 livres was close."

There follows in the letter a list of more than 100 books and periodicals, including several issues of some. The wide range of Lavoisier's interests at the age of twenty-four may be indicated by naming a few of the items he ordered: "History of the Academy of Berlin"; 12 drawings showing the clothing of ancient Strasbourg; "Acta of Physical Medicine," and books on light, acid and alkalies, heat, metals, alchemy, natural history, photometry, physical geography, and chemistry.

The trip back to Paris took the travelers through another part of the country; in all they had covered about 1,000 miles. Lavoisier was met by his father at Bourbonne-les-Bains on October 7th. There was much to talk over and still more to do in labeling and sending off to Paris the many specimens.

On October 19th, Lavoisier and Guettard arrived safely in Paris, to the great relief of Mlle Punctis. That night, although he was tired from the trip, Antoine did not forget to record the barometric reading, as he had done on every day of his journey.

After a month's vacation in Villers-Cotterets, Lavoisier

began arranging the material collected on the trip and preparing a report on the water analyses. Then he and Guettard started work on their geological map of France. When it was published—much later—by Monnet, Inspector-General of Nîmes, little credit was given to Lavoisier.

But the geological tour was otherwise a great success, adding both to his knowledge and to his growing reputation as a scientist.

# 4. SEEDS OF THE REVOLUTION

*When Antoine* was in his teens, his country was at war. The first open act of warfare had taken place far from the homeland, in the wilderness of America, where a part of the Ohio Valley was claimed by both France and England. The English were interested in driving out the Indians and establishing permanent colonies; the French were there as missionaries and fur traders, making friends with the Indians as they extended their claims by exploration.

In 1754, Governor Dinwiddie of Virginia sent a military expedition, under the command of a young surveyor named George Washington, to force the French out of the region that is now western Pennsylvania. But the French and Indians successfully defended their positions, and the next year soundly defeated the British General Braddock in his efforts to expel them. The American colonists were not too serious about taking the side of the mother country, many of them preferring instead to carry on a profitable trade with its enemy, France. Both European countries were having similar troubles in India, where each was trying to maintain a strong foothold.

At home, though pretending to want peace, the two governments were in fact looking around for military alliances, while the other continental countries were choosing sides. Hardly ten years had passed since the French army had been cut to pieces by the Austrian-British alliance, but when King George II of England attempted to renew the alliance, Maria Theresa, the Empress of Austria, turned him down. To recover the province of Silesia, which Austria had lost to Prussia by the treaty ending the previous war, she hoped to get France on her side. France itself was an open camp. To strengthen the country against England in the battle for colonies, some of the King's ministers favored joining Frederick the Great of Prussia; another group wanted an alliance with Austria. And while the haggling was going on, England made a secret treaty with Prussia.

Louis XV of France was easily swayed by the Marquise de Pompadour who was despised by the people as much for her extravagances and intrigues, as for her influence over the King in political matters. Madame Pompadour cared less about the welfare of France than about her own personal ambitions which she thought would be best advanced by friendship with Maria Theresa who, in turn, played her own game of flattering Louis and, of necessity, Pompadour, her helper at the French Court. Together they persuaded Louis to rid himself of the very ministers who had cautioned him against what turned out to be a fatal mistake, and before long France was plunged into war on the side of Austria—the Seven Years' War, which lasted until 1763.

France could ill afford a costly war, least of all one in which she would lose her colonial possessions abroad and impoverish the people at home. Although France was the richest country in the world, a great deal of her wealth was being squandered to support a fabulously luxurious Court: It is estimated that during his long reign, the yearly cost of maintaining the King's establishment was 40 million livres (about 80 million dollars).

In addition, the nineteen years that the Marquise de Pompadour ruled over Versailles cost the Court, according to her own account book, 75 million dollars. She owned over a dozen luxurious estates for her personal use, and a private theater, menagerie, and botanical gardens. Her stable at Versailles contained twenty-six carriage horses and every kind of carriage, each lined with expensive satins. One of her palaces alone cost 2,500,000 livres to build, and to run it she had fifty-six servants, including five cooks, two head porters, a wardrobe woman, three personal maids, three coachmen, three postillions (letter-carriers), four grooms, a huntsman, a torch-bearer, and a physician.

When the King married, 400 new palace positions were created, and when his son, the Dauphin, was seven years old, 100 additional servants were engaged to care for him.

The Court housed not only the royal family, their friends, and servants, but an untold number of nobles who had abandoned their estates to seek remunerative posts at Court. For example, the title of Gentleman of the Bed-chamber gave its holder the right to sell all powder for wigs, and perfume, used in quantities in a day when baths were considered unhealthful. The King's Equerry had the privilege of selling the Swiss Guards their uniforms. Another title-holder controlled the sale of the many thousands of candles used every evening. Even the ladies-in-waiting had their own special source of revenue: each morning they would collect the unburned candles from the night before and resell them at a handsome profit.

It is easy to see why the lazy, parasitical nobles fought for these posts, and why all kinds of jealousies and intrigues were a part of Court life. But where did all the money come from to support this stupendous waste?

The Court had various sources of revenue. Early in the eighteenth century, Louis XIV had established the "Royal Manufactures," a system of enterprises employing thousands of workers. Some of these were privately owned, but were run by means of subsidies from the government. Others, like the famous porcelain workshop in Sèvres and the Gobelin tapestry works in Paris and Beauvais, were government-owned and managed by government-appointed officials. These and other establishments—for making cloth, stockings, furniture, china, glassware—did a thriving business, mainly by satisfying the requirements of the Court and the nobility. A part of their profits also went directly to the government.

Another source of royal income was the sale of titles of nobility to merchants and other prospering members of the middle class. In keeping with this custom, Lavoisier's father bought such a title for him, on the occasion of his marriage. Though Lavoisier made little use of it, he was thereafter entitled to be referred to as "de Lavoisier." The wealthier and more ambitious paid for and received more imposing titles, granting them special privileges and at the same time bringing large revenues into the treasury's coffers. But the main source of government income was, of course, taxes.

Of all the evils that plagued France at this time, the worst was the unjust levying of taxes. For instance, the *vingtième*, or one-twentieth, levied on income and property, seemed on the surface to be a fair way to distribute the tax load; but it didn't work out that way. For one thing, the Church lands, though yielding enormous revenues, were exempt from taxation. Continuing the ways of the old system, the clergy stubbornly refused even to give an accounting of their income, to say nothing of giving part of it to the state.

Nor did the aristocracy produce anything of value to the country. Since they earned nothing, many nobles were unable to maintain their out-of-repair estates and lived at the expense of their peasants. Some lost their lands by deserting them for high posts in the army, the government, or the Court. Others sold out to the *bourgeoisie*, the wealthy members of the Third Estate, the only people in the country who had money. These men acquired prestige for themselves by buying titles or by marrying their daughters to impoverished noblemen, gradually taking over most of the worldly goods of the Second Estate. Thus, in one way or another, the nobles had lost their wealth and become parasites.

When the peasants, who made up the vast majority of the population of France, managed by hard work to reap a good harvest, more than half of their income was taken away by taxes. To the King went the *vingtième*, the *taille*, and the *gabelle,* the last being the most hated because salt was a prime necessity in the limited diet of the poor. The nobles exacted duties for the use of ovens, wine presses, granaries, and bridges. Then there was the *corvée,* or forced labor, to maintain the roads and the estates, stables, and households of the nobility. This work often had to be performed when the peasants should have been working their fields.

Yet for all the power and privilege enjoyed by the King, the nobility, and the higher clergy, the *ancien régime* was dying. The upper section of the bourgeoisie, the wealthy manufacturers and merchants, the bankers, financiers, and newly risen landowners, had become the leading group. They were no more loved than the nobility, and perhaps they were feared even more.

Especially was this true of the bankers, whose power rested on their ability to make loans to the manufacturers, the nobles, the merchants, and even the King. A century earlier, when the French had refused to pay their taxes, the King's minister had turned to the financiers. In exchange for a fixed payment of money each year, they were permitted to collect and keep the taxes on salt, tobacco, and wine.

This company of already rich men levied the highest possible taxes, impoverishing the people for their own profit. They were called Farmers-General, and their organization was the *Ferme Générale,* or Tax Farm. To be sure, some members (like Lavoisier, who later became a Farmer-General) were honest and well-meaning men who sought to reform the tax system. But because of their function as collectors, they became for the people the most hated single symbol of oppression.

The events of a losing war made matters worse. In 1757, an alliance was concluded with Austria, France's former enemy. Although it was opposed by the people and proved to be ruinous to the country, the indifferent Louis submitted to Madame Pompadour's scheme and joined Maria Theresa. By the terms of the treaty he agreed to impoverish France further by increasing her contribution of troops and paying a yearly subsidy to the Empress of Austria until Silesia was recovered from Prussia.

The French army suffered defeat after defeat. Led by one incompetent general after another, it moved into battle accompanied by baggage trains, empty of war matériel but filled with powder and perfumes and chefs and attendants for the vain and disinterested officers. Unable to enforce military discipline, the officers permitted the disorganized troops to become a mutinous mob, and in the fall of 1757, at the Battle of Rosbach, the army suffered a catastrophic defeat at the hands of a much smaller and weaker Prussian force. When Frederick of Prussia was asked how this could have happened, his ready reply was: "The French general has twenty cooks and not a single spy, while I have twenty spies and but one cook."

Still bound to the ambitious Austrian Empress, Louis refused every opportunity for a separate peace. As the war went from bad to worse abroad, both India and Canada were lost to England, while Frederick the Great still held Silesia. When, in 1763 the Peace of Paris was at last signed, England had become the strongest power in Europe, while France emerged from the war almost bankrupt, and with a loss of 200,000 lives.

Louis XV knew only one way to solve his problems: more and more burdensome taxes on his subjects.

## 5. YOUNG ACADEMICIAN

*The most* powerful group in the newly emerging order of society—the Third Estate—was also the most enlightened and liberal. It was represented by those intellectuals known as *philosophes,* spokesmen for this growing, prospering class of society. The *philosophes* ushered in the "Age of Reason," an intellectual revolution against everything that was old and outworn. Their influence was widespread, not only in France but in much of the rest of the world. They declared war on the aims and methods of the *ancien régime,* its ignorance, superstition, tyranny, and uncurbed privileges for the few. They stood for the principles of free opinion and the equality of all before the law, as well as for free industry, free labor, and free trade. They were opposed to the unquestioned authority of the clergy, and they denied the Divine Right of the King.

The *philosophes* were witty and eloquent, but they were also learned men, brilliant and profound. They were not only the philosophers—like Voltaire and Diderot—the writers, pamphleteers, playwrights, artists, scientists, and musicians of their day, they were also the great reformers. Many of their ideas for a better France were hatched in the gay and sophisticated salons of Paris.

Everybody who was anybody was part of this group of intellectuals. No one could afford to ignore them, not even the King and Madame Pompadour who were often forced to be on their side.

The *philosophes* were not rebels to the point where they would break with the King. So while Louis XV temporarily suppressed the *Encyclopédie,* ordering all existing copies of the first three volumes to be destroyed, and on many occasions imprisoned some of these open critics of his government, he also handed out generous pensions to others. And the pensions were accepted and even sought as a means of livelihood. Voltaire was known to have said, "I indeed love truth well, but I do not at all love martyrdom"; while Diderot declared, "to suffer martyrdom in any cause proves nothing, except that our party is not the strongest."

It was in this group of brilliant and forward-looking men that Lavoisier found his natural and rightful place as a scientist, statesman, and reformer. Here his intimates included Diderot and d'Alembert, editors of the *Encyclopédie*; Condorcet, the mathematician and economist; Rousseau, the political theorist and educator; Lafayette, the young general and ardent champion of the American Revolution; Turgot, the statesman, as well as some of his teachers, like Guettard and Rouelle. Among them were botanists, mathematicians, astronomers, and chemists, members of the Academy of Sciences, who saw unusual promise in the young Lavoisier. Membership in this body was a great honor. Only the best-known scientists could hope to be elected, and an Academician was highly regarded, both as a learned man and one who had done a great deal for his country. Antoine was believed to be a likely candidate for this honor.

While Lavoisier was still on his tour of northern France, plans were being made for his advancement as a scientist. The gold medal he had received for his work to improve the street lighting of Paris, his research on the different kinds of gypsum (a mineral from which plaster of Paris is made), and other papers he had submitted to the Academy put him in line for candidacy—at least so his friends thought. And now he was making a geological tour to prepare an atlas of France!

During his absence, many influential men visited Lavoisier's father, talking about his son's geological work, reading his letters, and looking forward to the successful completion of the project. In the course of the conversations they told his father how highly the young student was regarded by the Academicians.

The Royal Academy of Sciences had just celebrated its one hundredth anniversary. Established in 1666 by Colbert, Minister of King Louis XIV, its function was to advise the Court on scientific and other questions important to the development of the country. By its own rules the Academy was a highly selective society. The regular membership was limited to fifty-four, and not all had voting privileges. The highest rank was that of honorary member, and all twelve of those had to be noblemen. From this group, which served without pay, the president and vice-president were chosen by the King. The next rank consisted of eighteen *pensionnaires*, or paid members who received regular salaries from the government. Then came twelve associates and twelve assistants, making up the two lowest ranks. The only others were the retired *pensionnaires* and associates, and members from other countries.

Except for the honorary members, each rank had an equal number of scientists from six fields—astronomy, physics, mathematics, anatomy, botany, and chemistry. Vacancies occurred only on retirement or death of the members and could be filled only by persons in the same field of science. The two associates and three *pensionnaires* in the particular science prepared the list of new candidates who were voted on only by the two highest ranks. Finally, the successful candidate had to be approved by the King. For all these reasons, election to the Academy was not only a great honor, but also a difficult one to achieve. Even after election the assistants had no voting privileges, and had to take their places on hard benches behind the comfortable chairs occupied by the associates.

In 1766, Lavoisier's name was placed on the list of candidates awaiting a vacancy. The opportunity arose when a chemist member died two years later. Lavoisier was by this time a strong candidate. But his runner-up was a much older and more experienced scientist who was in charge of developing coal mining in northern France and was also the inventor of a method of manufacturing red lead, both important contributions to the development of French industry, meriting recognition by the Academy. So, though he enjoyed a wonderful reputation and his friends spoke well of him as a young, intelligent, and energetic man who could do much for his country, Lavoisier's youth—he was only twenty-five—was against him.

When it came to the election, Lavoisier received a majority of the votes. To satisfy everybody, Lavoisier's name and his opponent's were presented to the King with the novel recommendation that both be elected, and that no new election be held when the next vacancy occurred. The King agreed, and thus Lavoisier became an Academician almost at the beginning of his brilliant scientific career. An unheard of recognition for one so young! How proud and happy his father and Aunt Constance were that their beloved boy was granted an honor coveted by men twice his age.

The very next year, Lavoisier's friendly contender for the Academy post died. No election was held, and Lavoisier became a regular assistant in chemistry.

Long before this Lavoisier had lost no time in getting to work as an Academician. This was no social club, and there was plenty to do. The members met two afternoons a week for discussions, plans, and reports, but this was only a small part of the Academy's work. More like a government bureau than a "society," the Academy concerned itself with many practical problems of conducting the affairs of the nation, and especially those of its capital, Paris.

The Academy published annually a volume, called *Mémoires,* to which scientists contributed the results of their special work. Even before Lavoisier was considered for election, he had had four articles accepted for publication in the *Mémoires,* on such different subjects as the properties of gypsum and city lighting. The scientific papers were usually read before the Academy once a month, and then rejected or accepted for publication. There was also the job of editing and printing the *Mémoires.*

Lavoisier took part in this, as well as in many other problems considered by the Academy. Some of these concerned the welfare and expansion of the city of Paris: where to build the public slaughterhouse, how to provide a good water supply, how to heat homes and public buildings efficiently, how to deal with the foul odors from cesspools, and how to build an efficient pump and hydrant for fire protection. Others had to do with the development of industry—the working of mines, the manufacture of phosphorus, paper, ink, glass, sugar, starch, soap, the processes of extracting oils, the weaving of tapestries, the winding and dyeing of silk, the separation of gold from silver, the manufacture of lamp wicks, the making of charcoal from peat, the retting of flax to prepare it for spinning into linen.

Then there were questions of developing natural resources: locating the mineral deposits of the country, working lead and silver mines, obtaining alkali from mineral waters and sulphur from sulphurous springs. Other problems in which Lavoisier became involved were the adulteration of cider, the construction of smokeless grates, the engraving of coats of arms, making a vegetable rouge for the ladies of the Court, and—at the request of the city officials—how to explode fireworks!

However, not all of the technical matters that Academician Lavoisier worked on during his lifetime were immediately practical. While he was involved in the determination of weights and measures and tables of specific gravity, he was perhaps even more interested in fossils, meteorites, volcanoes, the effects of thunder and lightning, the breathing of insects, and even hypnotism.

The variety of subjects Lavoisier investigated would stagger today's specialist in chemistry or physics, but in his day it was different. Scientists—like Benjamin Franklin and Thomas Jefferson, Lavoisier's contemporaries in our country—showed their greatness in versatility rather than in specialization. Science was only in its earliest infancy, and specialists in a tiny area of one science were unknown.

Lavoisier put his ingenuity and knowledge at the service of his country, but had he been without the advantage of a wealthy family, and a personal fortune inherited from his grandmother, he might not have been able to give of himself so fully. To insure himself a lifetime income that would free him of the burdens of earning a living, Lavoisier made an important decision shortly after his nomination to the Academy of Sciences. He chose to join another, quite different, group of men. He bought a share in the *Ferme Générale,* becoming one of the Farmers-General.

This organization had nothing to do with farming or the army. As we have read, the Tax-Farm was a private company that collected taxes for the King, and its members paid the government for the privilege of collecting taxes, most of which they kept.

The Farm was organized into committees, each with its own job: one to collect the tobacco tax, one for the salt tax, one for keeping accounts, one for hiring and discharging the thousands of officials throughout France. Every Farmer-General worked on one or more of these committees, directing the affairs of the Farm. Lavoisier's intention in joining was to invest his fortune profitably and thus be able to give all his time to scientific research.

Not all of his friends thought it a wise move: they were afraid that the affairs of the Farm might take him away from his scientific work.

As the manufacturing class increased in size, so did the cities of France, and Paris most of all. Its population was increasing by leaps and bounds, but its public facilities, especially the water supply, did not keep pace with its growth. When Antoine was a young boy, he saw men and women taking water from the Seine and hauling it away in pails and barrels, on their backs or in horse-drawn wagons. Since the city's sewage and refuse drained into the river, the water was even then polluted, and by the time Antoine reached manhood, it had become a menace to the health of every inhabitant of Paris. Finally the Academy decided to study the problem, and engineering plans were drawn up for using springs and for getting additional and cleaner supplies of water from the Yvette River.

Ever since his geological survey, Lavoisier had been testing the density of different bodies of water. On the basis of his experiments he proposed to the city government a solution of at least one part of the problem: If a steam pump were set up to raise the water, and a system of pipes laid to distribute it, the people would be relieved of hauling the water to their homes. He carried his discussion to the public and soon his report was accepted by the Academy and the plan was put into operation. This did not, however, solve the problem of the need for pure water. Purification was not to be achieved for another century when the science of bacteriology was founded by another great Frenchman, Louis Pasteur. In the meantime the people of Paris had to boil all of their drinking water.

While housewives boiled their water, scientists at the

Academy meetings continued to discuss the old question of whether or not water turned into earth on evaporation. Lavoisier decided that the only way to find out was to experiment—talking would never settle the argument. By 1770 he was ready with a report of his experiments, later published in a series of articles called "On the Nature of Water and on the Experiments Alleged to Prove Its Transmutability into Earth."

"I wish to speak of facts," he wrote, and proceeded to tell how he had obtained the facts. He boiled rain water in closed glass and earthen vessels. Since all rain water carries dust and other particles washed out of the air, these small amounts of earth and salt settled to the bottom after boiling. He then took the clear water and distilled it, over and over. This he did by evaporating the water, condensing the steam into water by cooling, reboiling, cooling it again, and so on.

Lavoisier was then ready for the crucial part of the experiment, for which he had a carefully reasoned plan that included the proper apparatus. This consisted of the most sensitive scale he could obtain from the French Mint, a specially shaped vessel called a pelican, and a sand bath that could be gently heated with small lamp wicks. The pelican was made of two glass spheres (the bottom one large, the top one small) connected by a cylindrical neck. The top sphere had an opening that could be stoppered. He first weighed the empty pelican; then he filled the lower sphere with a weighed amount of water, and stoppered the opening at the top of the smaller one. He then set the vessel in the sand bath, just deep enough to permit the water level to remain visible. Great care had to be taken to free the pelican of the air as it expanded with the heat, or else the experimenter took the risk of breaking the glass. When at last all the air was forced out, the stopper was sealed off and the experiment was on its way.

For over 100 days the water was gently heated at a little below the boiling point. For a long time no change was visible, but after about a month fine particles, visible with a hand lens, appeared on the surface of the water. More and more tiny flakes reached the top. After several more weeks they settled, and no new ones appeared.

It was now time to find out what had happened. The wicks were removed, and the pelican was allowed to cool. The pelican and the water with its deposit of earth were weighed separately. The pelican had lost weight—not much, only 3/100 of an ounce—but enough to show on Lavoisier's extremely sensitive scale. The weight of the residue recovered from the water was approximately equal to that lost by the pelican, while the water weighed the same as at the beginning of the experiment. What did this mean?

Lavoisier concluded that the "earth" had come from the glass vessel, and not from the water. And what did this prove? That water was not converted or transmuted into earth! The "earth" had formed from the continued destructive action of the water on the glass! Thus Lavoisier destroyed a theory that had been held for twenty centuries, and was still believed by some of his friends in the Academy.

Beginning with a practical problem of the Paris water supply, Lavoisier ended with the solution to a scientific problem that had been argued fruitlessly for years. In 1770, as a result of his laborious and brilliant experiment, he could speak of a fact—water does not change into earth on evaporation.

# 6. LAVOISIER TAKES A WIFE

*Lavoisier* was now a busy and important man. What with committee meetings and trips of inspection to nearly every corner of France for the Tax-Farm, working on scientific problems for the Academy, writing papers and reporting to Academy meetings, and experimenting on his own, his time was fully occupied. Through the Academy and the Farm, his circle of colleagues and friends had enlarged, and soon he began to take part in the important social affairs of Paris. But for a long time his life did not include friendships with any women outside of the family —his beloved Aunt Constance and the devoted grand-aunts in Villers-Cotterets.

Among his newly acquired friends was Farmer-General Jacques Paulze de Chastenolles. A prominent lawyer and statesman, a wealthy widower, a director of the French and East India Company, and the father of a young but nonetheless marriageable daughter, M. Paulze was bound to attract the best of Parisian society to his home. Like other well-known people, he often held *soirées,* or social evenings, and entertained in style. And who could be a greater asset to his guest list than the brilliant young scientist who was the son of that highly respected lawyer, Jean Lavoisier?

After all, Antoine had been brought up in his grandmother's drawing room; he was at home at social gatherings and contributed to their success. He frequently attended the *soirées* of M. Paulze, who admired him greatly, and there Lavoisier met such men as Turgot, who later became Minister (Controller General of Finance); Pierre Du Pont de Nemours, whose son Irénée later came to America, where his descendants were to establish the world-famous chemical firm of Du Pont de Nemours; Benjamin Franklin, then visiting France on a mission for the American colonies.

In the company of these men, Lavoisier had much to give—and much to gain. He took a keen interest in political affairs and, stimulated by the brilliant discussions, he attracted attention and won many admirers by his easy and clever conversation.

A passport issued to him some years later described him as five feet eight inches tall, with brown hair and eyes, a long nose, small mouth, round chin, and thin face. Portraits of him show Antoine as a handsome man. His attention was eagerly sought by the ladies who gathered at M. Paulze's house. But it wasn't long before his interest centered on his host's pretty young daughter, brown-haired, blue-eyed Marie Anne Pierette. Though not yet fourteen when she met the distinguished young Academician, who was twice her age, she was already a young woman. The only daughter in a widowed household (she was only three when her mother died), she had matured early. Marie's head barely reached Antoine's shoulder, and a small pastel sketch, which later occupied the place of honor in Lavoisier's study, shows how attractive she was, with her quiet and serious expression and her slightly turned-up little nose.

Antoine was not the only interested young man. Others also wrote many a love letter to Marie. But her attention was only for Antoine. Wide-eyed, she would listen by the hour to his discussions with her father's guests. This did not escape M. Paulze, but he had no objection to Antoine as a son-in-law. Far from it. Was the young man not brilliant, handsome, renowned in science, and conscientious in his work for the Tax-Farm? Was he not from a prominent family, and wealthy besides? A most eligible bachelor!

Among Marie's many suitors there was the Count d'Amerval, old, good-for-nothing, and penniless. His sister, the Baroness de la Garde, had set her heart on arranging a marriage for him with Marie, who was both pretty and rich. Marie heartily disliked the Count whom she regarded as a "stupid, ill-mannered fool."

Finding the girl's father no less opposed, the Baroness enlisted the support of Abbé Terray, Marie's grand-uncle, who tried to persuade M. Paulze to give his daughter in marriage to the Count. The Baroness also tried to lure

Marie herself with the prospect of leaving her convent school and being presented at Court with lavish ceremony.

Terray, at that time Minister of Finance and one of the most powerful men at Court, threatened Paulze with expulsion from his post as director of the tobacco department in the Tax-Farm, and only his reputation as a competent official saved him. At this time, Paulze wrote to his uncle: "M. d'Amerval is fifty, my daughter is only thirteen; he has not even 1,500 francs a year, and my daughter, although not wealthy, can at this moment bring twice as much to her husband. His character is not known to you, but that it cannot please either my daughter or you or myself, I am, indeed, well assured. My daughter has a decided objection to him; I will certainly not force her against her wishes."

Meanwhile he thought and acted quickly. In November 1771, he arranged the marriage of Marie to Antoine. The signing of the marriage contract a few weeks later was as formal a ceremony as the signing of a state document. Two hundred guests, including Farmers-General, members of the Academy, the mathematician d'Alembert, and the botanist Bernard de Jussieu, who knew Lavoisier from his student days, witnessed the signing. Aunt Constance, proud and happy for her Antoine, was the first to sign, a privilege she well deserved.

The young couple scarcely had time for courtship. There was little opportunity for them to be alone, to take walks or go on outings, or to make plans for their future life together. The marriage took place on December 16, 1771, less than a month after their engagement. Granduncle Terray became sufficiently reconciled to act as witness at the marriage ceremony, which took place in his private chapel.

The Count and his disappointed sister were soon forgotten as Antoine and his bride settled down in their house, a present from his father, on the Rue Neuve des Bons-Enfants. They lived here only four years, but for more than 100 years the house was a landmark of Paris because of its association with the name of Lavoisier. Today the site is occupied by the Bank of France.

Even though the marriage had been arranged hastily to escape an unhappy union with a disreputable old nobleman, Antoine and Marie loved each other dearly, and their marriage was a most happy one. Madame Lavoisier was devoted to her husband, not only as a wife but as a scientific assistant as well. An excellent student, she was determined to become familiar with her husband's work and to learn Latin and English. This proved to be a great help to Antoine, who was not as good at languages as his wife, and he depended wholly upon her to translate scientific works written in English. Among her translations were two important books by the Irish chemist Richard Kirwan, and it is clear from the "Translator's Notes" that she understood the technical work as well as the language.

Drawing was another of her accomplishments. Marie had been a pupil of Jacques-Louis David, whose portrait of Antoine and Marie in Lavoisier's laboratory is famous. (David's painting is today in the possession of the Rockefeller Institute for Medical Research in New York.) Marie's ability as an artist was as useful to her husband as her knowledge of science and languages, for she made the drawings which illustrate Lavoisier's book, *Traité*

*Elémentaire de Chimie.* She was also his laboratory assistant, making notes as they worked together, and she acted as his secretary, taking care of much of his correspondence.

Apparently the Lavoisiers enjoyed music, for they had a box at the opera and both of them played the piano. Antoine even wrote a treatise on harmony.

Lavoisier had many friends and acquaintances, but no intimate friends. His closest associations were within the circle of his own family—his beloved father and his aunt and Marie. Antoine and his wife were a devoted couple. The catalogue of an art exhibition found among his papers after his death has, in his handwriting, this note on a painting that showed Alcestis restored to her husband by Hercules: "Either this man is not married or I pity him. He has never felt the joy of reunion with a loved one after separation."

Many distinguished foreigners as well as Frenchmen visited their home. On these occasions Marie enchanted her guests, entering into the conversations not only as a charming hostess, but as Antoine's scientific partner. One gentleman took exception to Madame Lavoisier's learning. Gouverneur Morris, who later was United States Minister in Paris, wrote in his diary on June 8, 1789: "Dine with Mr. de Lavoisier. . . . Madame appears to be an agreeable woman. She is tolerably handsome, but from her manner it would seem that she thinks her forte is the understanding rather than her person."

On September 13, 1787, Arthur Young, the British agricultural economist, who visited the Lavoisiers on his trip to Paris, wrote: "To M. Lavoisier by appointment. Madame Lavoisier, a lively, sensible, scientific lady, had prepared a *déjeuner anglais* [English breakfast] of tea and coffee, but her conversation on Mr. Kirwan's 'Essay on Phlogiston,' which she is translating from the English, and on other subjects which a woman of understanding that works with her husband in his laboratary knows how to adorn, was the best repast."

When Benjamin Franklin returned to Philadelphia, he wrote to Marie, thanking her for her kindness and hospitality, and on October 23, 1788, in a letter to Antoine, he referred to a portrait Madame Lavoisier had painted of him as one that "is allow'd by those who have seen it to have great Merit as a Picture in every Respect; but what particularly endears it to me, is the Hand that drew it."

Lavoisier had good reason to be proud of his wife as well as to be grateful for her help and devotion. Even without the fun young people usually have in getting acquainted before marriage, Marie and Antoine had a rich and happy life together, working side-by-side to develop the exciting new science of chemistry.

# 7. PROBLEMS WITHOUT END

*Like any* young married couple, during the first few months after their wedding Marie and Antoine learned to enjoy their life together and had fun in arranging their home to suit themselves. When spring came they spent their holidays in the country, often visiting Villers-Cotterets, the scene of so many of Antoine's happy vacations with his family. On their picnics in the woods, every path and shaded brook, always dear to Antoine, was now something to share with Marie as he recalled his childhood days. Then there were visits with his father and Aunt Constance, and to friends living on nearby estates.

Everyone was delighted with Antoine's little bride, her grace and quiet friendliness captivating all who met her. But just as all lovely things must end, so did their first summer together, and it was once more time to work on the many problems facing Antoine in the city and the Academy.

There was, for instance, the mystery of the disappearing diamonds. This is *not* a tale of stolen treasure. It *is* the story of the first really important work Lavoisier did in chemistry. In the middle of the eighteenth century the problem of what happens when a substance burns was by no means understood, and was far from being solved. Lavoisier was ultimately to solve it, and his diamond experiment was the beginning of the answer.

According to the English chemist Robert Boyle, whose theory had lasted for more than a hundred years, diamonds were "destroyed," or "evaporated," at high temperatures. Now Lavoisier had a genius for raising questions, many of which he answered through carefully planned experiments. So it was not unusual that he should ask: did the diamond evaporate, or did it burn? He was determined to settle this problem, over which there was so much violent disagreement among the Academicians.

One of the people who believed that diamonds (which are a form of pure carbon), unlike rubies (which are a metallic salt), evaporated under great heat was Lavoisier's old and beloved teacher, Rouelle. He and his son-in-law had recently heated diamonds and, like so much charcoal, the stones had burned completely. But, Lavoisier asked, suppose all air was excluded while heating them—then what would happen? He had an idea that air was important in the process.

Not everyone thought that diamonds would burn. Among the disbelievers was a jeweler by the name of

Maillard, who was so confident that he offered three of his own diamonds for the experiment. He did set one condition: that he be present to make sure his diamonds would be protected from the air. Lavoisier himself had one other condition: the diamonds must be carefully weighed before the experiment.

All previous experimenters had used an open vessel over a very hot furnace fire. Lavoisier had a different idea. He would use the heat of the sun concentrated on the gems by a giant lens. The Academy owned a lens that had originally come from Germany. This was placed in the noonday sun in a spot in the Jardin de l'Infante behind the Louvre.

Lavoisier enlisted the help of three men, Cadet, the oldest and most respected chemist, Macquer, whose laboratory diamonds had been heated in a furnace, and Brisson. When they started to work, they found that the lens, which had been gathering dust for two generations in the Academy's collection of equipment, was not strong enough. But when another lens, four feet in diameter, was added to it, the sun's rays were focused with intense heat.

After being weighed, the three diamonds were packed into a clay vessel filled with powdered charcoal and then sealed with more clay, so that no air could reach the gems. The lenses were then turned so that the sun's rays were directed at the diamonds. After being exposed to this piercing heat for some time, the vessel was opened. The diamonds were intact and only slightly discolored! Again they were weighed on the same scale. They had lost none of their weight. None of the material had evaporated!

Lavoisier had proved that *if air was excluded* the diamonds did not disappear. Air was needed for burning!

It would seem that since the diamonds, sealed off from air, remained intact after long and intense heating, everyone would have been convinced by the experiment. But not everyone was, least of all Lavoisier's old chemistry teacher. Rouelle fumed with anger, clinging to the old idea that diamonds evaporated with heating. There were even nasty rumors that Lavoisier had cheated; it was whispered that either the heat wasn't sufficiently great or the experiment hadn't been continued long enough. There is no greater scientific crime than cheating in an experiment, and Antoine was understandably deeply hurt, especially since some of the criticism came from people he respected and loved, like the now aging chemistry demonstrator who had taught him so much. But Lavoisier did not flinch from the criticism. He was unhappy about his professor's disapproval, but it did not shake his own belief in the facts he had discovered.

Yet the story of the disappearing diamond was not complete; the mystery of its evaporation was still unsolved. What became of the diamond when it was subjected to the same intense heat, but *in air*? Did it just disappear, or did it change into something else? Lavoisier hoped the second part of his experiment would provide the answer.

This time he permitted air to come in contact with the diamonds. But he also arranged his apparatus to make possible the collection of any other "air" that might be formed. (In those days the word *air* meant the same thing the word *gas* means today.) It took only twenty minutes for the diamonds to vanish in the sun's lens-focused heat. And a gas *had* been formed. What was this "air"?

For the answer to this question, let us start by going back several years to a young Scottish doctor and chemist named Joseph Black. Dr. Black was trying to find a way to dissolve kidney stones in some of his patients. He started with a mild alkali–known then as white magnesia –and chalk which contains calcium carbonate. Other alkalies were also well-known, such as the soda and potash used in soap-making, and quicklime produced by heating either limestone or chalk in a kiln.

When he heated limestone and white magnesia, Dr. Black found that both lost weight. He assumed they had lost "air"–which, however, he did not collect–and he called it "fixed air," because he at first believed it to be ordinary air "fixed" in the mild alkalies. Later, Black noted that when limewater was exposed to ordinary air it became covered with a crust of white chalk; he concluded, correctly, that the change was caused by a *different* kind of "air." (Today we call this "air," or gas, carbon dioxide.) Continuing his experiments, Black showed further that this gas was produced when charcoal was burned and when grapes fermented in wine-making. He also found it to be present in air expired by animals and man (if one breathes into limewater, it turns a milky white).

Dr. Black became so involved in his work on "fixed air" that he forgot all about kidney stones, and in 1764 he performed another unusual experiment. One day, in the city of Glasgow, 1,500 people attended services in a certain church for ten continuous hours. From the church's ceiling the doctor hung a vessel containing soda lime (a mixture of limewater and caustic soda). Air from the 1,500 pairs of lungs became mixed with the rest of the air, and a part was taken up by the soda lime, turning the latter a milky white. (Calcium carbonate had been precipitated, a combination of limewater and carbon dioxide exhaled by the worshipers.) However, since the same precipitate was formed as a thin crust on the limewater when it was exposed to ordinary air, Black concluded that the latter also must contain "fixed air."

Joseph Black discovered his "fixed air," formed as charcoal burned and as animals breathed, a dozen or more years before Lavoisier performed his diamond experiment. But this simple idea was contrary to everything that chemists in Lavoisier's time believed. They thought there was only one air, with or without a mysterious ingredient known as *phlogiston.* According to this theory, fully accepted by most scientists, all combustible substances contained an element of fire or inflammability called phlogiston—from the Greek work meaning "to burn"—and when a substance burned, its phlogiston escaped. Substances which burned almost completely, leaving very little residue, were supposed to contain a great deal of phlogiston. Thus oils and candle tallow were said to contain more phlogiston than hard coal because the coal left more residue when burned.

No one had ever seen, smelled, tasted, weighed, or measured phlogiston, but anyone who dared to dispute its existence and doubted the theory was a heretic in the realm of eighteenth-century chemistry. People believed that there was good air and impure air; that the latter was loaded with phlogiston, but that if it were "dephlogisticated" it became pure air again.

Even Joseph Black did not question the phlogiston theory. Unable to grasp the meaning of his own experiments, he failed to recognize that the fats, charcoal, and other substances he burned *were changed into a new kind of gas*, the one we now call carbon dioxide.

The gas collected by Lavoisier when he burned the diamonds in air was none other than "fixed air." It is to the credit of Dr. Black that he accepted Lavoisier's explanation: like the soft dull charcoal, the hard brilliant diamond was a "combustible body." Though strikingly different in appearance, charcoal and diamonds were identical in behavior in that both burned in air and both were changed to a gas. Once again, with a single experiment, Lavoisier had swept aside an old and false notion—that diamonds had mystical properties. They were just burnable substances, a single chemical element.

Of course, Lavoisier made many enemies by demonstrating that water was not transmutable into earth, and that diamonds burned like other fuels. Again there were criticisms and arguments, but these only steeled him against his critics. Through continued searching experiments he was to blaze many more trails in the new science, clearing up the morass of mistaken ideas held by the chemists of his time.

That same year (1772) Lavoisier bought an ounce of phosphorus from a pharmacist, and on September 10th he wrote in his notebook that he planned to find out whether or not phosphorus absorbed air when it burned. Perhaps he chose phosphorus because it oxidizes so readily in air that to prevent it from disappearing, even without heating, it must be kept under water. Also, as was usual with him, he may have wanted to start with something that already had been done but not fully explained to his own satisfaction. He knew, for example, that Stephen Hales, an English clergyman, had noted that phosphorus took up lots of air when burned; but Hales, like Joseph Black, had not understood the process.

In a note sent to the Academy on October 20th, Lavoisier reported that burning phosphorus absorbed large quantities of air, forming an "acid spirit of phosphorus" (we call it phosphoric acid), and gaining weight as a result of the combination. Twelve days later he deposited a sealed note with the Secretary of the Academy, with the request that it not be opened until he was ready to reveal its contents. What were his reasons for doing this? Was he unsure of his conclusions, and therefore unwilling to risk criticism if the results were not correct? Or, if he thought he was on the right track, did he want to insure that he would be credited with a discovery before any one else? Whether one or both of these reasons motivated him, the action revealed something of Lavoisier's character: he always had to be sure of his facts, and he was jealous of his claims to scientific discovery.

Six months later, when the note was opened and read before the Academy, his reason was clearly stated, along with the description of his results. The note read, in part:

> "I discovered that sulphur, in burning, far from losing weight, on the contrary gains it. . . . from a pound of sulphur one obtains much more than a pound of vitriolic acid [sulphuric acid] . . . it is the same with phosphorus; this increase of weight arises from an abundant quantity of air

> that is fixed during the burning and combines with the vapors. This discovery, which I have established by experiments . . . has led me to think that what I have observed in the burning of sulphur and phosphorus may well take place in the case of substances that gain in weight in burning. . . .
>
> "I felt that I ought to secure my right to it [the discovery] by depositing this note in the hands of the Secretary of the Academy, to remain sealed until the time when I shall make the experiments known."

Basing his conclusion on facts alone, and proving it by experiment, Lavoisier had made the then revolutionary discovery that phosphorus and sulphur, and perhaps other substances, combine with air while burning. This was the beginning of his explanation of combustion, an idea which he was later to extend and make more exact—namely, that during the combustion of substances, *only one part* of air combines with them.

At this same meeting Lavoisier reported that the "fixed air" which escapes from burning substances is entirely different from the ordinary air we breathe.

The problems Lavoisier was called upon to solve some years later were by no means all in the field of chemistry. They were as varied as they were numerous. To all of them he brought an open mind, a questioning attitude, a searching for facts. The facts were subjected to testing and retesting, and once established they were interpreted according to the brilliant reasoning for which he became increasingly noted.

The problems which Lavoisier took part in solving were so varied that several actually had less to do with science than with magic. Because people had not yet outgrown their belief in the powers of the alchemist to make gold, to furnish an elixir of life that would make old men young, and to cure the hopelessly ill, they were the gullible victims of many charlatans who had a field day until their paths crossed that of Lavoisier.

At that time, and even today, water-divining, or "dousing" as it is called in some places, was widely believed to be a rare and prized skill which only certain "psychic" individuals possessed. Since there was no sure way of knowing where water would be found, people who had to dig wells relied on a water-diviner to locate a plentiful supply. The douser used a "divining rod," a forked stick (shaped like the letter Y), usually cut from a willow or pear tree. Grasping the two forks of the branch firmly, with the backs of his hands facing in and with the main part of the branch extended in front of him, the douser walked slowly over the land. When the rod pointed downward, even against the diviner's strongest resistance, that was where the well-digger went to work. And he usually found water.

The Duc d'Ayen had met a famous water-diviner. He wrote about him to Macquer who, in turn, brought the whole question to Lavoisier, an expert on matters of water supply. Lavoisier, skeptical of anything that smacked of magic, was only too anxious to put water-divining to the test.

After he had talked it over with several members of the Academy, a spot was selected for the experiment. The chosen area was almost completely surrounded by a stream of water. The diviner was blindfolded and taken to the spot, where he carefully paced up and down and across the ground. His divining rod failed to dip here, there, or in the next place. Then suddenly he claimed that it was pointing to the exact spot where water was to be found. But when his blindfold was removed, to his great chagrin and discredit, there was water all around, not only where he had "found" it with his magic rod!

Lavoisier had proved his point: Water may very well be found wherever one wishes to believe it is located. He then wrote to the Duc d'Ayen that there was water in most places, and that it was rare to dig a well and not find water more often than not. "Many persons of good faith are often thus deceived," he commented, explaining that the motions of the wand were not spontaneous, but depended upon the movements of its carrier.

Before long the Academy was presented with another important problem. This time the government requested an investigation of the claims made by an Austrian physician who, after touring Germany with his "cures" of the lame, the halt, and the blind, was taking Paris by storm. The authority of Parisian physicians was being threatened by this man, Dr. Friedrich Anton Mesmer, whose "animal magnetism" was supposed not only to cure, but to spread from the healthy to the sick. The treatment, called "mesmerism," consisted of gripping an iron bar or applying it to the diseased part of the body. Often several patients were treated at the same time. With hands linked, they sat in a row of chairs while music played and the mesmerizer passed the "magnetic" rod before their eyes or around the affected parts of their bodies. At some time during the "magnetism" session, the patient was supposed to go through a "crisis" which differed in different people. Some coughed, screamed, hiccoughed, or rolled on the floor with laughter. Others fainted or became convulsed, while the "animal magnetism" supposedly coursed through them. After the "crisis" they were "cured." But it also often happened that patients remained perfectly calm through the procedure, and underwent no crises.

In 1784 the Academy appointed a commission of several members, including Lavoisier and Benjamin Franklin, who was then in Paris. It was Lavoisier who drew up the report of the commissioners' observations. In it he indicated their reluctance to judge the efficacy of any cure. The wisdom of their skepticism was expressed in these words: "Nature, left to her own devices, cures a great many diseases; and when remedies have been applied, it is extremely difficult to decide how much is due to Nature and how much to the remedy." Where medical cures were concerned, evidence could be considered valid only when a large number of cases had been studied, not merely a single instance.

Because the Academicians were not physicians, they did not pass judgment on the remedy itself, but confined their tests only to the existence of "animal magnetism." To this end they submitted themselves to "mesmerism" as practiced by one of its disciples, Dr. Deslon of Paris. Since none of them experienced anything resembling a crisis, they suggested that perhaps the patient's imagination and belief in the method had a great deal to do with the "cure."

Experiments were then set up in Franklin's house in

Passy, outside Paris. When the patients were blindfolded and told they were being "magnetized"—even though they weren't—many went through a crisis. Then, still blindfolded and after the crisis, they were again "magnetized"; this time they remained calm and steady! A whole series of planned experiments with objects that were supposed to be "magnetized" by Deslon's method, carried out on blindfolded or otherwise unsuspecting patients, proved beyond the shadow of a doubt that there was nothing to "mesmerism" that could not be explained by the imagination, or by what we today would call the power of suggestion. The commissioners condemned the practice as a hoax and a fake, harmful to the persons who let themselves be "treated" by it.

Thus not only in constructive work, but in exposing charlatans and quacks, Lavoisier applied clear logic and experimental testing.

# 8. BUILDING THE NEW OUT OF THE OLD

*It has* often been said that Lavoisier discovered no new substances, and that he leaned heavily on the work of others. Probably he himself would have been the last to deny this. With the utmost thoroughness he studied the experiments of his forerunners and kept in close touch with the work of his contemporaries, both in and out of France. His greatness lay in his unusual ability to devise experiments to test the results of other scientists' work and to interpret and explain the facts. Where others collected the facts, but lacked the understanding of their significance, Lavoisier was able to give them meaning. This was especially true of his work on combustion, dealt with in his first major publication, *Opuscules Physiques et Chimiques* (Physical and Chemical Essays) which appeared in 1774, two years after his experiment with the diamonds.

Lavoisier devoted the greater part of this book to an historical review of experiments with air and its separation from various substances. Thoroughly familiar with the work of the English chemists on gases, he employed many of their methods, improving on them with more exacting techniques. Since some of these reports were written in Latin and others in English, Marie was undoubtedly of indispensable help in making those in English available to him in the French language.

To understand fully Lavoisier's contribution to the new chemistry, it is necessary to know what he inherited from his predecessors, for this was his starting point. Closely tied up with his experiments on combustion, and reported in the same sealed note to the Academy, was his work on the *calcination* of metals. (The early chemists used the word "calcination" to describe what we call *oxidation*, but their observations on the process came long before the discovery of oxygen, of which they were completely ignorant.) Lavoisier recognized early in his study of oxidation (or calcination) that somehow—as in burning—air played an important role.

Exactly a century before Lavoisier read his report to the Academy on the burning of phosphorus and sulphur, Robert Boyle had published his *Essays on Effluviums* in which he described his experiments with various metals heated in open crucibles: tin, lead, copper, and iron changed their properties from those of metals into those of more or less soluble powders called *calces*. Some, like iron, required no heating to change into the *calx* or, as we would say today, to be converted into rust, or the *oxide* of the metal. Moreover, Boyle, had shown that the calx always weighed more than the metal from which it was produced. What was the cause of this gain in weight? Boyle thought it was due to particles of fire absorbed by the metal. A different explanation was offered by another Englishman, John Mayow, who attributed the gain in weight to what he called "nitro-aerial" particles from the air. This explanation came nearer to our present understanding of the process of oxidation—a combination of the metal with oxygen from the air.

The correct theory of burning might have come a century earlier but for another idea, one that was very slow in dying. This was the *phlogiston theory*, originated during the seventeenth century by Johann Joachim Becher, and extended by another German, Georg Ernst Stahl. As we have seen, according to this theory all inflammable substances contained the common element phlogiston, which was lost when they burned. As proof, it was pointed out that when the calx of a metal was heated with a combustible substance such as charcoal, the calx was changed back into the metal while the charcoal disappeared. This was true of course, but what was the explanation? According to the phlogiston theory, the phlogiston of the charcoal passed to the calx, restoring it to the original metal. Therefore, it was argued, a metal was a calx combined with phlogiston, from which it followed that metals were, like charcoal, combustibles. The supporters of the phlogiston theory represented their idea in this simple equation:

$$\text{Metal} = \text{calx} + \text{phlogiston}$$

The idea was plausible enough, but there was a fly in the ointment, the unexplained fact that the calx weighed more than the metal. If it had lost its phlogiston, the metal should have weighed more than its calx, but the scales clearly showed the opposite. Lavoisier's contemporaries tried to explain this in many complicated ways, in fact in any way that would fit in with the phlogiston theory. Some chemists said, for instance, that phlogiston was lighter than other substances, that it had "negative" weight; so while other matter was pulled toward the earth, phlogiston rose toward the heavens. But Lavoisier saw only the glaring discrepancy: Since metals *gained* weight on calcination, how could they have *lost* something —phlogiston or anything else? Not satisfied with the accepted explanations, he planned a number of experiments of his own.

Using both the burning lens and an open fire, he heated a mixture of charcoal and red calx of lead. Collecting the expanding gas, or "elastic fluid" as it was then called, over a vessel containing water covered with oil (to prevent the gas from dissolving in it) he trapped it in another vessel filled with water and inverted over the first vessel. In one experiment he reported that the volume of the gas was 747 times greater than the lead which remained after heating the mixture of charcoal and red lead.

Next came the examination of the gas, and here again he turned to the experiments of Joseph Black who had obtained a gas (his "fixed air") by pouring acid over chalk. The test for "fixed air" was the same whether it was released by treating chalk with acid or by reducing a calx to its metal. In each case the gas snuffed out lighted candles, dimmed the glow of burning charcoal, killed animals that breathed it, and turned limewater milky. Of course, Black's "fixed air" and Lavoisier's "elastic fluid" were one and the same gas, the one we know as carbon dioxide. Here are Lavoisier's comments contained in his sealed note:

> "I am persuaded that the increase in weight of metallic calces is due to the same cause [the taking up of air]. Experiment has completely confirmed my conjectures: I have carried out the reduction of litharge [calx of lead] in closed vessels, with the apparatus of Hales [by which the calx of lead was heated with charcoal], and I observed that, just as the calx changed into metal, a large quantity of air was liberated and that this air formed a volume a thousand times greater than the quantity of litharge employed."

While Lavoisier confirmed Boyle's experiments with the calcining (oxidation) of metals, he went beyond the latter's observation that the calces (oxides) weighed more than the original metals. His own conclusions, carefully reasoned out on the basis of his laboratory results, combined a number of important new points:

The calcining of metals required air, or some part of it, since the process failed to occur in vessels in which all the air was exhausted.

The elastic fluid (gas), released when calces were reduced with charcoal, was "fixed air."

The greater the amount of metal that was exposed to air, the greater was the amount of calx formed.

Boyle's conclusion that the gain in weight of the calx

came from absorption of fire particles through the pores in the vessels was wrong, Lavoisier noted. And this is how he backed up his criticism:

If the calcination was done in sealed bottles, weighed before and after heating, the weight of the total did not change. If, indeed, particles of fire were absorbed, and the precaution of weighing the sealed vessels before and after heating was followed, the vessels' weight would have increased, but the experiment did not show this. What actually happened in the sealed vessels was a reduction in the amount of air by exactly the amount gained by the calx. When the seals were broken after calcination, the outside air rushed in with a noise, replacing the consumed air. At this point the total apparatus weighed more than at the beginning, so that the increase in weight was due to the additional air, not to particles of fire.

At the end of the year 1774, Lavoisier read his report on calcination before the Academy, and shortly afterwards it was published in a journal called *Observations sur la Physique* (Observations in Physics). Again criticism was directed at Lavoisier, but of a different kind from that following his experiment with the diamonds. On the very day he read his paper, a letter was dispatched from Turin, Italy. In it the Italian physicist, Father Beccaria, informed Lavoisier that some fifteen years earlier he had himself demonstrated that the calcining of a metal (tin) in a closed vessel depended on the size of the vessel, and that the total weight of vessel and contents remained the same throughout the experiment, there being at the same time a reduction of the quantity of air in the vessel.

Despite his custom of reading all reports of experiments

that had been done before his, Lavoisier apparently had missed Father Beccaria's work, although it was in the *Memoirs of the Turin Academy.* Naturally disappointed at learning that he had only repeated previous work—which could easily happen because at that time communications between scientists were far from adequate—Lavoisier was at the same time glad that his own findings had been confirmed. In any case, he did the expected thing; included with his paper to the journal was a letter to the editor, in which Lavoisier stated:

> "It concerns me that the public should be convinced as soon as possible that I have no mind to appropriate to myself another man's results; and I am convinced that propriety in literature and science is no less essential than in morals. Although the experiment of Father Beccaria somewhat lessens the novelty of my experiments, I declare to you that his letter has given me great pleasure and that I am delighted to see adopted and confirmed by a celebrated physicist the theory of the increase in weight of metallic calces which I thought I had been the first to develop."

But the matter of the Italian's priority of discovery did not end with Lavoisier's acknowledgment of Beccaria's work. Another Frenchman, Pierre Bayen, was working with the calx of mercury, which he had reduced *without* the addition of charcoal. In the course of his investigations he had dug up a century-old book of essays by Jean Rey, describing similar experiments on the calcination of metals, and publicly referred to them in a letter to the journal *Observations*. Bayen could not himself claim credit for the work, but he reproduced the results of the forgotten physician, perhaps mainly as a taunt to Lavoisier.

In the end Lavoisier duly acknowledged the experiments of Boyle, Rey, and Beccaria, all of which antedated his own. But important as these results were historically, they fell short of Lavoisier's. The others had observed, noted, and recorded their data as isolated experiments whose meaning they either guessed at or failed to explain correctly. Lavoisier was the first to furnish final and conclusive proof that the gain in weight by oxidized metals was due to air. More important, this series of experiments was but a link in the chain of a revolutionary new theory of combustion and respiration which Lavoisier both envisioned and ultimately worked out to completion.

# 9. GUNPOWDER

*In 1774*, after a reign of fifty-nine years, Louis XV died, a victim of the disease that had claimed so many of his subjects—smallpox. His twenty-year-old grandson, Louis XVI, ascended the throne. He was the new ruler of France, but a sorrier figure, fat, awkward, and pudgy-faced, never wore royal robes in France's fabulous, polished Court. He was all the more conspicuous against the grace and beauty of his wife. The marriage, arranged by Louis XV and Maria Theresa, Marie Antoinette's mother, had made the young Hapsburg princess the Queen of France.

More than anyone, Louis himself wished he were not king. He realized that he had neither the ability nor the desire to tackle the affairs of his country, and he much preferred to ride, hunt, and pursue his hobby of making and repairing locks. Timid, weak, and capricious, without a mind of his own, he was happy to leave governmental matters to his ministers, to his frivolous, extravagant Queen, and to the selfish courtiers who surrounded her.

The finances of France, managed by the Farmers-General, were in a sad state. Most of the taxes collected were eaten up by the provisions and pensions for the Court favorites and the royal family who lived in extravagant luxury. Out of necessity, Louis entrusted the management of financial affairs to a new Minister, Turgot. An able and upright statesman, the Controller General of Finances immediately set about making reforms in the Tax-Farm and its management.

The first problem Turgot attacked was that of gunpowder production. This was being handled by a private company, organized like the Tax-Farm, and under contract to furnish 1,000,000 pounds of gunpowder a year. But there was a hitch: If it failed in its contract, or if there was a national emergency (like the Seven Years' War), there was nothing the government could do except to buy gunpowder, at a great cost, from other countries.

The chief ingredient of gunpowder was saltpeter (potassium nitrate) obtained by digging in stables, pigsties, sheepfolds, and pastures where cattle grazed. The company's workers had the right to dig for saltpeter anywhere, and were entitled to free lodging and transportation from the digging grounds to the powder factory. The landowner had to bear this expense as a patriotic duty; but if he could afford it, he would pay the diggers to stay off his land. In this way the saltpeter-diggers often made more money by not working!

To make its product, the company also needed fuel,

for gunpowder was the result of heating a mixture of saltpeter, lime, and wood ashes. The fuel used was wood, and no matter where it was gathered the villagers had to supply it at a set price, as well as to furnish free lodging to the woodcutters. The company's monopoly included not only saltpeter for munitions, but all gunpowder used for hunting and blasting, including that sold outside France. Of course, the company made huge profits, but it avoided paying the government the money called for under the contract.

Turgot set out to correct this deplorable situation. In 1775, he organized a Gunpowder Commission, made up of four members who put up 4,000,000 livres (approximately $8,000,000) to buy out the private company and continue the manufacture of gunpowder for the government. In return for his investment and services, each member was to receive 2,400 livres a year, with additional payments according to the amounts of powder the Commission produced. Lavoisier, who as a Farmer-General enjoyed a reputation for honesty, ability, and industry, and whose knowledge of chemistry was invaluable in this work, was appointed a Commissioner.

His job was clear-cut: He must increase the saltpeter without burdens to the people, but with a profit to the royal treasury. From now on, free transportation for the diggers was abolished, and the landowner had the right to bargain for the cost of wood and saltpeter obtained from his property.

In less than a year the work of the Gunpowder Commission showed amazing results. The yield was increased, the advance to the Commissioners was paid off, and there was a profit of 900,000 livres. Farmers and villagers no longer wanted to get rid of the diggers, as they were now able to bargain for the sale of their saltpeter and so had an interest in increasing the available supply.

But these improved conditions were only a part of Lavoisier's contributions to the solution of his country's munitions problem. On his advice, artificial niter beds were set up (as they had been in other countries), and the Academy was instructed by Turgot to offer a prize for the best plan on the preparation of saltpeter. As usual, Lavoisier was made a member of the committee appointed to put the plan into action, and in 1777 he edited a report of the Gunpowder Commission on the construction of niter beds and the manufacture of saltpeter.

Meanwhile, in 1776, Turgot had been dismissed as Minister. His reforms didn't please Louis' corrupt courtiers. Lavoisier continued in charge of the Grand Arsenal. Under his direction the production of gunpowder steadily increased; its quality improved and it was being produced at a much lower cost. Whereas formerly the government had to buy saltpeter from foreign countries, 1,500 Frenchmen were now employed in its manufacture. In fact, France began to export gunpowder, to such an extent that it became the main source of supply for the American colonies in the Revolutionary War.

His appointment to the Gunpowder Commission meant a change in Lavoisier's personal life, too. With this government post went living quarters, a beautiful house, with the convenience of being close to his place of work. So, four years after their marriage, Antoine and Marie left their home in the Rue Neuve des Bons-Enfants and moved into the Arsenal where they lived until 1792. Here he also set up a laboratory and worked on his many chemical problems. For nearly twenty years the home of the Lavoisiers—and their laboratory—was a meeting place for many prominent scientists, including Benjamin Franklin and James Watt, the inventor of the steam engine.

In the autumn of 1775, Jean Antoine Lavoisier died suddenly at his country home at Le Bourget. The loss of his father was a great blow to Antoine. As he himself said, "It is less the loss of a father that I mourn, than the loss of my best friend." Now Marie became all the more his close companion and co-worker, sharing his risks and troubles as well as his successes.

In his researches on gunpowder, Lavoisier traveled all over France, prospecting for sources of saltpeter, while in his laboratory he conducted experiments on its production. One of these experiments nearly cost both his life and Marie's. It was in 1788, and he was trying out a newly discovered ingredient—potassium chlorate—as a substitute for saltpeter. The morning the new gunpowder was to be tested, the Lavoisiers, and M. Berthollet, who had discovered potassium chlorate, drove to the factory. After making arrangements to mix the explosives in a small mortar outside the building, and instructing the workers to stay behind a screen to protect themselves, they left to have breakfast. Just as they were preparing to return, they heard an explosion, and hurrying back to the factory they found both mill and mortar wrecked. The workers who had remained behind the screen were safe, but the manager and a woman visitor who had failed to heed Lavoisier's instructions had been killed.

In spite of this unfortunate incident, Lavoisier believed that the work was worth while, and he reported to the

Minister of Finance thus: "If you will deign, sir, to engage the King's attention for a moment with an account of this sad accident and the dangers I faced, please take the opportunity to assure his Majesty that my life belongs to him and to the state, and that I shall always be ready to risk it whenever such action may be to his advantage, either by a resumption of the same work on the new explosive, work which I believe to be necessary, or in any other manner."

At the opening of the French Revolution, Lavoisier was a member of the Gunpowder Commission. On August 6, 1789, a quantity (about 10,000 pounds) of low-grade gunpowder, manufactured in Metz and intended for export, was in the Paris Arsenal on its way to the ports of Rouen and Nantes. Pressed for storage space, the Commission decided to forward it immediately to Essones where it would be exchanged for musket powder that Paris could always use in the event of a Royalist uprising.

All shipments of munitions had to be approved by the Commander of the National Guard, Lafayette. At the moment he was not available, so his Chief of Staff, La Salle, signed the order. But when a number of citizens saw the powder being loaded for transportation and so informed the local authorities, Lafayette—not knowing that the shipment had been authorized—ordered that the boat be unloaded. This confirmed public suspicion that there was foul play, and the Gunpowder Commission, headed by Lavoisier, was accused of robbing the people of their ammunition.

The National Assembly sent two representatives to investigate. They ordered the powder returned to the Arsenal where four barrels, picked at random, were opened in their presence and that of Lavoisier. It was a low-grade powder. Lavoisier's calm explanation of the situation was accepted, but later, when other accusations were being leveled at him, the incident was recalled and held against him.

# 10. THE DISCOVERER WHO MISSED

If *Lavoisier* had not put his keen mind to work in interpreting the discoveries of others, the importance of the most abundant element on our planet—oxygen—might well have eluded scientists for many more decades. As it was it took two men, separated geographically by the English Channel and following two completely different paths, to discover the element and explain how it is necessary for all life. However, Joseph Priestley and Antoine Lavoisier did have one thing in common: a consuming desire to understand the physical world. In their quest for truth, they met only briefly on one chance occasion, but that meeting provided the spark needed to light the road on which Lavoisier was to travel to his final conquest of the problem.

In the discovery of oxygen, and in the demonstration of its universal significance, not only in chemistry but to all living things, the work of these two men is so closely interwoven that to appreciate Lavoisier's contribution fully, we must also understand that of Priestley. For this our story moves to England, Priestley's homeland.

When Antoine Lavoisier was an infant, Joseph Priestley was ten years old. He was born in 1733, the oldest of six children, in Fieldhead, England, noted for its cloth-dyeing industry. His father was a cloth-finisher, and his mother was a farmer's daughter. When Joseph was only six years old his mother died. Several years later he was adopted by his aunt, Mrs. Keighley, who took care of him as her own child. Shortly after Joseph went to live with her, Mrs. Keighley's husband died and left most of his considerable property to his widow who, according to Priestley, "never spared herself" to do good.

Mrs. Keighley's home was a gathering place for dissenters, Protestants whose interpretation of Christianity was different from that of the established Church of England. The dissenters living in the neighborhood came to Mrs. Keighley's and the nearby Independent Chapel "to worship in spirit and truth." There they were welcome, whether for public meeting, conversation, or prayer, and the young Priestley had many opportunities to listen to discussions on religion, politics, and philosophy. These meetings were a far cry from the social gatherings in Madame Punctis' drawing room where Antoine heard so much stimulating talk of events in France. Joseph's life was grim, empty of the fun that boys usually enjoy. He spent his Sundays in prayer and meditation, and during his holidays there were no carefree excursions, no games, no wanderings in fields and woods. Instead young Priestley learned Greek, Latin, and Hebrew. Books were almost his only recreation.

But the boy enjoyed his reading, although it was on serious subjects, for he hoped to prepare himself for the ministry, even though he stammered, a handicap in such a profession. At the age of sixteen, he contracted what was probably a mild tuberculosis, and had to curtail his studies. He dropped the dead languages and applied himself to French, Italian, and Dutch, learning them without the help of an instructor. Later, while teaching Hebrew to a minister, he also learned Chaldee, Syriac, and Arabic.

Besides languages, he learned geometry, algebra, and grammar, but no science. When, much later, he became interested in science, he learned all he knew about it at home, by reading and working in his own amateur, homemade laboratory.

As a dissenter, and one with little money, he was excluded from all but the small schools supported and run by local church congregations. Nevertheless, when Joseph entered the Nonconformist Academy at Daventry, he was so much more advanced than the other pupils that he was excused from the first-year studies. Languages were omitted from the curriculum, but he continued to study them, getting up earlier than the others to read by himself or with a schoolmate. In the academy students rose at six and attended prayer sessions until it was time for breakfast at eight. Before supper there was prayer again, and bed at ten o'clock. The academy gates were kept closed and discipline was strict, with fines as punishment for breaking the rules.

On leaving the academy, Priestley had two occupations open to him—preaching or teaching, and these in the poorest churches, supported only by the meager funds of the parishioners. His first salary was thirty pounds a year (about $150) of which twenty went for his board. But he had never been interested in money, devoting himself with fervor to his ministry and to teaching the parishioners' children. As a schoolmaster he took the greatest pains with his thirty boys and six girls, whom he taught in two separate rooms, and after school he tutored private pupils.

He arranged for a collection of books and encouraged his pupils to read. He taught them to write original compositions, and even wrote a book on grammar to simplify their language work. After his appointment, in 1760, to the Warrington Academy, he thought a great deal about methods of education and wrote *An Essay on a Course of Liberal Education for Civil and Active Life*, published in 1765. Here he stated his ideals for an education to fit young people for life, business, and service to their country. In another of his works, dealing with his own teachings in history and civil policy, he discussed three forms of government—aristocracy, monarchy, and democracy—and showed his own liberalism by favoring democracy.

Three years before this, in his thirtieth year, Priestley had married Mary Wilkinson, the daughter of a parishioner whose younger son was his pupil. He described his wife as a "woman of an excellent understanding, much improved by reading, of great fortitude and strength of mind, and of a temper in the highest degree affectionate and generous; feeling strongly for others, and little for herself." Mary Wilkinson did not have the charm or attractiveness of Lavoisier's Marie, and certainly had no interest in her husband's later scientific work, but she was nevertheless a good wife to Joseph, with whom she lived happily.

At the academy the teachers and their families formed a congenial community, meeting for Saturday afternoon teas and parlor games. Priestley was happy during these years, enjoying the warm companionship of his small circle. He also had one hobby—he learned to play the flute and played it often for his own amusement and relaxation.

During this time he occasionally visited Manchester, Liverpool, and London, where he had friends with whom he carried on learned discussions. On one of his trips to London he met Benjamin Franklin who for a number of years was the English agent of the American Colonies, and who was largely responsible for getting the Stamp Act repealed. Some years later, while in France during his country's struggle for independence from England, Franklin was also to meet Lavoisier.

Priestley at this time was no scientist but, having attended a few lectures in elementary chemistry in the academy, he became fascinated by that science. Even before that, while teaching in the parish school, he had bought a few scientific instruments with his meager savings, setting up an air pump and an electric machine, whose workings he demonstrated to his pupils.

Franklin was known in Europe not only as a diplomat and ambassador but as a scientist of distinction, welcomed in the universities and meetings of learned societies. Priestley's interest in electricity was quickened by his meeting with Franklin who gave him some books on the subject. He studied the books, and within a year, in spite of his many duties as teacher, writer, and minister (he was ordained in 1762), he completed a *History of Electricity*. As a result of this, he was elected in 1766 to the Royal Society of London. The year before he had been granted an honorary degree by the University of Edinburgh in recognition of his book, *Chart of Biography*. He was now Dr. Priestley, with a degree in Letters, and a member of the Royal Society, but he was still a poor, struggling teacher and minister.

In 1767, his salary being insufficient to support his growing family and ailing wife, Priestley leaped at the opportunity to become the minister of Mill Hill Chapel at Leeds. Strangely enough, this post was to lead to the beginning of his fame as an experimenter and great discoverer. Near his new home there was a brewery, and here, during every spare moment, Priestley could be found bent over the fermenting mixtures in the great, smelly vats, a strange occupation for anyone, especially for a preacher.

During the process of beer-making, gas bubbles escape from the surface of the brewing mixture. Priestley noticed that when he set fire to chips of wood and brought them close to the bubbles, the flames were extinguished. So absorbed was he in his observations that he never noticed the snickers and amused expressions of the brewery workers as they exchanged glances behind the queer minister's back. He probably wouldn't have been disturbed even if he had been aware of them, for he was too engrossed in trying to answer the question: what was this gas that put out the flame of his burning chips?

He had an idea that it might be the "fixed air" Joseph Black had seen escaping from heated limestone, and that if he could capture enough of the bubbles, he could really find out. Working at home, he learned how to prepare and collect enough of the gas to study its properties. In this way he found that when just enough of the gas was dissolved in water it gave it a "pleasant sparkling taste which could hardly be distinguished from seltzer water." In fact, he prepared a weak solution of carbon dioxide in water, the same thing that gives the sparkle to the soda water of our modern "soft drinks."

The discovery was important enough to interest the Royal Society before whose fascinated members he bubbled the gas through plain water. After the learned scientists had tasted the sparkling, mildly acid solution, Priestley was awarded the Society's gold medal. It was even thought that the drink could be used as a remedy for scurvy which plagued British sailors, and it was recommended to the Admiralty by the College of Physicians.

This, the first of the amateur scientist's triumphs, gave him the needed encouragement to pursue his experiments in chemistry. And what greater diversion could there be from his quiet life as a minister?

In 1772 he published his paper on "Directions for Impregnating Water with Fixed Air," and from here he went on to releasing other gases and to inventing a method to collect them over mercury. This method made possible his discovery of a hitherto unknown gas which, unlike carbon dioxide, was highly soluble in water. Earlier scientists had failed to collect it, because the gas was absorbed by the water in their vessels. But in Priestley's experiment it was trapped in a flask of mercury inverted over a dish filled with the same element, which it displaced as he produced it by heating table salt with sulphuric acid. A first-year chemistry student today can write the chemical equation for this reaction in symbols not even invented in Priestley's time:

$$2NaCl + H_2SO_4 = 2HCl + Na_2SO_4$$

(Sodium chloride + Sulphuric acid = hydrochloric acid + Sodium Sulphate)

Hydrogen chloride (Priestley's "marine acid air") dissolves readily in water to form hydrochloric acid (which he called "muriatic acid"). The colorless gas with its strong, irritating odor, has many uses in modern industry.

Nor did Priestley stop here in his absorbing hobby. He also collected "alkaline air" (ammonia) in the same way. It didn't matter to him that sometimes he couldn't catch his breath because of its irritating vapors, or that they made his eyes burn. He had found another "air" soluble in water, now so important to all of us in cleaning fluids, refrigerators, and air conditioners. Quite often he didn't know what he got, nor did he plan his experiments with any special idea in mind, but his interest never flagged; he was a careful observer, and the results never escaped him. He combined the two gases, hydrogen chloride and ammonia, just to see what would happen. To his great surprise they formed a white cloud that settled in the dish as a white powder. He had discovered ammonium chloride, a powder, something completely different from the two reacting gases and without their odors. Today it is indispensable in the manufacture of dry-cell batteries, and is useful in medicine.

After each new discovery, Priestley enthusiastically went on to the next, soon isolating nitrous oxide (he called it "nitrous air"), which he later used to test the "goodness" of air. The more the experimenter labored in his home-made laboratory, seemingly forgetful of family and parishioners, the more his congregation became alarmed over what seemed to them an unbecoming zeal—in a minister—for science.

That Priestley's new absorption in science did not diminish his devoutness, but only confirmed him in his religious beliefs, can be seen from the preface to one of his earlier volumes on Air. In it he states that the growth of knowledge can only serve to remove ignorance and bigotry where *both* religion and science are concerned. It is possible that he was trying to appease the grumblers in his parish, but it is far more likely that the honest Priestley meant every word he wrote.

Meanwhile, using both the pneumatic trough he had invented to collect soluble-in-water gases over mercury and the device by which earlier scientists had collected insoluble ones in a flask inverted over a trough of water, he went on experimenting. He tried heating solids with the biggest burning lens he could find—a foot in diameter. The lens was not as large as Lavoisier's, for Priestley didn't have the expensive laboratory equipment available to his French contemporary, but while heating one of these substances—a red powder called mercuric oxide—he made the most important discovery of his life, one that was to make him one of the most famous of the great chemists of all time.

The experiment seems simple enough today. He placed the mercurous calcinatus (mercuric oxide) in a bell jar, and arranged the burning lens so that the heat of the sun was concentrated on the powder. After heating, he found that the mercury remained, while the escaping gas was collected (through a tube) in a bottle placed over a trough of mercury. "I presently found," he wrote, "that air was expelled from it readily." So far there was nothing remarkable about his experiment, for others had collected gases from decomposing chemicals.

Then, quite by chance, he reached for the candle on his table and placed it in the bottle. Unlike the gas escaping from the fermenting beer vats, this gas did not extinguish the candle. On the contrary, it burned with greater brilliance than in air! He put a red hot iron wire in the bottle, and it glowed and sparkled. Charcoal also, as if fanned with a bellows, quickly burned out.

Priestley was beside himself with wonder and excitement. The minister-turned-chemist had freed oxygen, but he did not recognize it! The fact that he was not a trained scientist was the least of the reasons why he failed to realize what he had discovered. The most important reason, the one that made him stubbornly blind to his dying day, long after his own and others' experiments had revealed the truth about oxygen, was that he was hopelessly immersed in the phlogiston theory. He was sure that the gas was not a simple element in the air, but a compound of phlogiston, earth, and nitric acid.

Priestley believed that all air was supplied by volcanoes, and that it was originally inflammable. Burning fuels and living animals added phlogiston to it, he thought, and growing plants removed it, making the air again fit for breathing. When he placed a sprig of mint in a glass jar, inverted over a vessel of water, he noticed that the mint grew. The air inside the jar did not extinguish a candle, nor did it kill a mouse exposed to it.

So he concluded that the air in the jar had become restored, or "dephlogisticated," making it possible for a flame—and life—to survive in it.

A year passed before he performed another experiment that would have interested, and certainly would have puzzled, the brewery workers if they had seen the odd minister at his strange occupation. For two years he had spent a part of the winter as librarian and companion to Lord Shelbourne who lived alone in his castle in Bowood near Calne. One night—to kill time in the cheerless castle—Priestley set out traps for mice, wire cages from which he could easily remove them alive. The next morning he filled one flask with oxygen and another with ordinary air, inverting them both over water. In each flask he placed a mouse, on a little platform where it would be safe from drowning. Then he sat down, watchfully waiting and playing his flute, having no idea how long the experiment would last.

But it wasn't long—less than a quarter of an hour—before he put his flute aside. Mouse number 1, in the air-filled flask, slumped and fell unconscious. In fact, it was dead when he pulled it out. But its companion, breathing oxygen, was still alive! You can imagine with what suspense the minister watched the little captive in the oxygen flask: how long would it take before it too would succumb? In another fifteen minutes it too quieted down, its eyes somewhat bleary and its fur moist, and then it collapsed! But he removed it in time, warming it by the fire until it revived and once more became active. Priestley could hardly believe what he saw. The first mouse had died in fifteen minutes, while the second was still alive after being a captive twice as long.

Was it only an accident? He repeated the experiment, with the same results. Assured that it wasn't a matter of chance, and that the air in one flask must be more wholesome than that in the other, Priestley reasoned that perhaps the former was the "nitro-aerial spirit," discovered a century before, and so-called because it turned arterial blood bright red. He decided to breathe some of it. After inhaling some freshly prepared gas through a glass tube, this is how he described his sensation: "I fancied that my breath felt peculiarly light and easy for some time afterward. Who can tell but that, in time, this pure air may become a fashionable article in luxury. Hitherto only my mice and myself have had the privilege of breathing it."

Priestley dreamed of many uses for this refreshing gas he had discovered. He thought it might help people who had lung trouble—and, indeed, it is today used not only for victims of polio, pneumonia, and heart disease, but for people saved from drowning and suffocation, for high altitude flyers, and for mountain climbers, like the courageous conquerors of Mount Everest. He even foresaw the possible dangers of breathing it as a "steady diet": "For as a candle burns out much faster in this air than in common air, so we might live out too fast. A moralist at least may say that the air which Nature has provided for us is as good as we deserve." But he still didn't know that his wonderful gas was oxygen.

History, however, has queer turns. In 1774, even before Priestley had performed his experiments with the mice, Lord Shelbourne invited him on a trip to the European continent. While in Paris he met Lavoisier, an event that was to prove even more fruitful than his enjoyable and well-earned holiday.

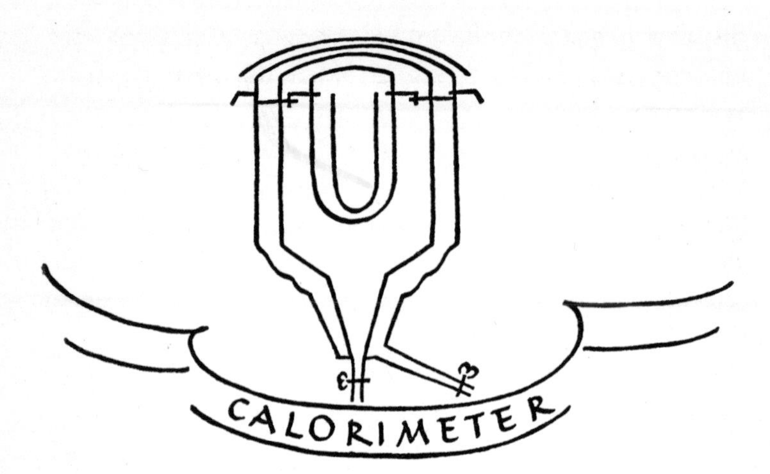


# 11. THE REVOLUTION IN CHEMISTRY

story of oxygen

*Even with* his many duties in the service of the government, Lavoisier found time to continue his chemical experiments, working particularly with mercury calx, a substance in which many other chemists were interested at the time. Most calces (metallic oxides) could not be reduced to the metal without the addition of charcoal. When the mixtures were heated the charcoal was used up, showing that the "air" given off in the reduction was a combination of the gas separated from the metal and that given off from the charcoal. Mercury calx, however, could be reduced without charcoal, so Lavoisier selected it as the most suitable for his next experiments.

He reasoned somewhat in this way: If mercury calx is heated with charcoal, the gas formed is "fixed air." It dissolves in water, snuffs out fire, precipitates in limewater, and kills animals that breathe it. When the same substance is heated *without* charcoal, the gas *does not* dissolve in water and *does not* precipitate with limewater; moreover, it will combine again with the metal, and make burning wood splinters sparkle and animals lively. He concluded, therefore, that this gas, which combined with the metal and increased its weight, was *pure* air, ordinary air in its *pure* state. Thus far he had proved nothing more than Priestley had, but he explained what he found *without using the phlogiston theory*. He was convinced, instead, that the answer was to be found in air, air in its *pure* state, as he said.

One might ask if Lavoisier would have gone on with his experiments if Joseph Priestley had not paved the way. As a matter of fact, this question was debated for years, but really without much point. Far more important is the way the story of oxygen actually unfolded.

Priestley's fame as a researcher had gone before him. Honored by the Royal Society of England, he was accorded the welcome he merited by the Parisian chemists in October 1774. The modest minister-turned-scientist was now among his equals, and those who had read of his work were eager to greet him. For his part, Priestley wanted nothing more than to meet the French philosophers and men of science who were interested in the same problems that occupied him. Of them he said: "They are a set of philosophical men, whose object is freedom of commerce and universal peace." In turn, their great regard for him surprised and delighted Priestley: "They could not possibly show more respect to anybody than they did to me, especially on account of my 'Observations on

Air' which have engaged the attention of almost all the philosophers on the Continent."

Among those with whom he had lively conversations were Macquer, Condorcet, Cadet, and Berthollet, but most of all it was Lavoisier whom he sought out. A frequent visitor at the Lavoisier home during his stay in Paris, Priestley enthusiastically observed and recorded the experiments Lavoisier performed. And, of course, there was a great deal of talk about his own experiments. "I mentioned it at the table of Mr. Lavoisier when most of the philosophical people of the city were present, saying it was a kind of air in which a candle burned much better than in common air, but that I had not then given it any name. At this all the company, and Mr. and Mrs. Lavoisier as much as any, expressed great surprise," Priestley later wrote.

Apparently Lavoisier was not only astonished, but found much to ponder over in Priestley's results. It was at this time that he decided to repeat the mercury calx experiments. Where Priestley failed to see that his gas had something in common with the air of the atmosphere —after all, it formed the oxide when heated *in air*—Lavoisier proved it by showing that even in the absence of charcoal the oxide could be formed. Viewing these findings in the light of the older theory, Priestley believed that since the new air was many times better than ordinary air, it must be free of phlogiston.

When the mutually profitable visit was concluded, both men returned to their laboratories, Priestley taking back to England a sample of red calx of mercury supplied him by the French chemist Cadet. Lavoisier was also to use a sample of the same material. Early the next year (1775)

Priestley performed his experiment with the mice, and on March 15th he reported his discovery in a letter to the Royal Society. Published in *Philosophical Transactions* a week later, the letter announced publicly and for the first time the discovery of the new, highly respirable air.

After Priestley's return to England, Lavoisier lost no time in devising his own experiments with mercury calx. On April 26, 1775, he read his report before the Academy of Sciences. The title, "On the Nature of the Principle which Combines with the Metals during their Calcination and Increases their Weight," suggests that his talks with Priestley a few months earlier had borne fruit. It was clear from this report that he was now convinced the gas was the pure stuff of the atmosphere, and that it was recovered from the calx by reduction.

For two more years Lavoisier worked on this problem, repeating Priestley's experiments again and again, as well as working with tin and lead calces heated in sealed, air-tight vessels. The total weight of the containers remained the same before and after calcination. Only when the seal was broken, and the vessels were filled with *more* air, did they show an increase in weight. Lavoisier was sure that the increase came from the air, since it was almost, though not quite, the same as the gain in weight of the metal itself. Moreover, the density of the part that combined with the metal was almost, but not quite, the same as that of air: it was *heavier* than both ordinary air and the air left behind after calcination.

On the basis of these observations, Lavoisier came to his history-making conclusion: *The air of the atmosphere was not a simple substance, but a mixture of two different substances!* One of these was respirable, supported combustion, and made possible calcination (rusting, or oxidation); the other was not respirable, did not rust metals, and did not support combustion.

With this explanation, Lavoisier moved far ahead of where Priestley left off: The substance discovered by Priestley was not "dephlogisticated air," but just one part of ordinary air, with newly discovered properties.

Lavoisier went on from these experiments to study animal respiration. After making a calx by heating mercury for twelve days in a closed vessel, he measured the sealed-in air; it had lost approximately one-sixth of its volume, and would snuff out flames and asphyxiate animals. He then heated the calx, and recovered the one-sixth of the air lost during calcination; it supported both burning and breathing. Then, by having animals breathe in a confined space, he found that "fixed air" (carbon dioxide) was formed as a result of their respiration. Somehow, ordinary air was changed into "fixed air," and this was breathed out. On the other hand, the nonrespirable part—which he called *moffette* (meaning asphyxiation), and which is now known as *nitrogen*—passed through the lungs unchanged.

The process of respiration, Lavoisier reasoned, must be like burning: Heat is given off and, just as charcoal burns in a stove and heats a room, fuel is burned in the body, giving it its steady temperature.

By 1778 Lavoisier was ready to present to the Academy his complete findings on air—the fact that it was made up of two parts, and the role it played in the rusting of metals and the burning of fuel. During calcination, he reported, the gain in the weight of metals was due to "nothing other than the healthiest and purest part of the air." The air released by heating mercury calx was "purer than the very air in which we live." When mercury calx was reduced with charcoal, "fixed air" was given off. This was due to the combination of charcoal with what he called the "pure part of the air," and it was "eminently respirable."

Lavoisier went on to explain some of his earlier experiments: When phosphorus was burned, it combined with this special air to form "acid of phosphorus," and under the same conditions sulphur yielded "vitriolic" (sulphuric) acid. In fact, he said, *all* acids contain this air, and he named it oxygen, from two Greeks words meaning "to give birth to acid." (This idea of Lavoisier's was incorrect, but that is how oxygen got its name.)

In modern chemical language we would write Lavoisier's conclusions in this way:

> Metal + Oxygen = Metallic oxide
> Carbon + Oxygen = Carbon dioxide
> Heating metallic oxides releases oxygen
> Mercuric oxide burned with charcoal (carbon) yields mercury and carbon dioxide, as the charcoal is consumed. In respiration, fuel is burned with oxygen, and carbon dioxide is given off. Air is composed of oxygen (respirable) and nitrogen (irrespirable)

It all seems simple today, but in Lavoisier's time the leading chemists could not accept the new theory. Their thinking had been clouded for so long by the idea of phlogiston as the "fire principle," that their minds could not acknowledge the clear explanation offered by Lavoisier.

Perhaps he was not an originator, but he had the genius for giving scientific meaning to the experiments of others, as well as his own. He was so far ahead of all his contemporaries that it took years for the others to catch up with him. And when that time arrived, the phlogiston theory was dead and buried, slain by the genius of Antoine Lavoisier.

In the experiments by which he discovered oxygen, Lavoisier only touched on the subject of respiration and animal heat. True, he showed that when ordinary air was breathed in, "fixed air" was expired, and he thought that living animals thus maintained a steady body temperature higher than that of their surroundings. As we have seen, he concluded that this must be due to the release of heat in the lungs as oxygen was changed into "fixed air," and that the process was no different from the burning of charcoal in air.

Lavoisier always checked his reasoning with experiments. In this case he set himself the task of finding a way to measure both the heat and the fixed air. But how could the "matter of fire" (heat) be measured? Once more he turned to an experiment done by Joseph Black some twenty years before. Black had shown that when ice melts (changes to water), it takes up heat. Since this heat cannot be measured with a thermometer, because the surrounding water remains at 32° Fahrenheit, the freezing temperature, he called it "latent [or hidden] heat." This gave Lavoisier an idea of how to go about measuring the heat animals give off. Needing a suitable apparatus, he called on the mathematician Pierre Simon de Laplace to design it, and together they carried out a series of experiments ending in 1784.

The apparatus was called an ice calorimeter. It was a large vessel, like a pail, divided into three circular compartments, one inside the other. In the innermost compartment one could put a heap of burning charcoal, or a live animal. In the middle one there was a weighed amount of ice. The outer compartment was packed with snow, to keep the ice from melting with the heat of the room. The experiment had to be suspended in the summertime because, without mechanical refrigeration or dry ice (neither yet invented), there was no way to prevent the ice from melting.

The idea behind the experiment seems simple to us today. As the charcoal burned, its heat melted the ice—the more intense the heat, the greater the amount of water that formed. The burning charcoal melted 10½ ounces of ice. In the same way a guinea pig, completely unaware of its role in a great historic experiment, sitting on its haunches inside the iced compartment, melted the ice around it. In ten hours' time, the heat of the guinea pig melted 13 ounces of ice.

But this was only half of the experiment. Lavoisier and Laplace also found a way to measure the "fixed air" (carbon dioxide) freed at the same time. In a separate apparatus they collected and weighed the "fixed air." They could then calculate the amount of heat produced from the amount of "fixed air" collected. This proved to be very nearly the same amount as that measured by the melting of the ice. The guinea pig liberated 236 grains

(1 grain equals 1/7000 of a pound) of "fixed air" while the charcoal released 224 grains.

The burning of food by the live guinea pig and the burning of charcoal were identical processes—and the amounts of heat, "fixed air," and oxygen could be *measured*! This was proof, indeed, that combustion and respiration are similar: both require oxygen, and both liberate carbon dioxide as well as heat. The heat given off by the guinea pig came from the burning processes in its body, heat which maintained its body temperature at the same level. As it lost heat, more was being formed by its tissues to replace the loss. This is how Lavoisier described it: "Thus the air that we breathe serves two purposes equally necessary for our preservation. It removes the fixed air from the blood, the excess of which would be harmful; and the heat that this combination sets free in the lungs makes up for the continuous loss of heat to the surrounding atmosphere."

The experiment, of course, was important for its immediate results and for the explanation of oxidation in animals (with the exception that heat is not released by the lungs). In addition, by this work Lavoisier paved the way for the study of other chemical reactions in which heat could be measured. His and Laplace's was the first calorimeter, the pattern for the modern, extremely complicated instruments and the forerunner of the calorimeter that measures the latent heat of all kinds of fuels and foods, and the heat produced by animals and human beings.

Lavoisier and Laplace wrote the first chapter of the story of what happens to food in the body, and explained the basic process of burning. Thus, too, they made clear not only what breathing is, but the role oxygen plays in the "furnaces" of the body. For the first time it was shown that breathing is not just a cooling of the lungs by fresh air—it is a chemical process. These experiments were the first ones on metabolism.

Lavoisier went on, some years later, to measure the amount of oxygen a man breathed at work and while resting, with and without food, in a warm room and a cold one, in winter and summer. For these experiments, Lavoisier's young friend Armand Séguin replaced the guinea pig. Séguin wore an airproof leather mask and breathed oxygen through a tube. The amount of oxygen he breathed in an hour was carefully recorded, while Marie Lavoisier drew pictures of the process and the apparatus. In one picture Séguin is sitting quietly; in the other he is doing work by pressing a pedal with his foot.

When the experiments were complete and the figures recorded, the experimenters drew up the following table:

| *Condition* | *Temperature in the room* | *Oxygen absorbed per hour in cubic inches* |
|---|---|---|
| AT REST | | |
| 1. Without food | 77° Fahrenheit | 1210 |
| 2. Without food | 54° " | 1344 |
| 3. With food | 54° " | 1800–1900 |
| AT WORK | | |
| 4. Work without food | 54° " | 3200 |
| 5. Work with food | 54° " | 4600 |

The results showed that a man uses more oxygen when he is working than when he is resting, more when taking food than fasting, more when it is cold than when it is warm. The more heat he gives off, the more oxygen he uses in burning more fuel. Work requires not only more air, but more food.

"Why, in shocking contrast, does the rich man enjoy an abundance which is not physically necessary, and which seems appropriate to the man of toil?" Lavoisier commented. "Let us beware, however, of calumniating Nature and of blaming her for faults that, no doubt, originate in our social institutions and are perhaps inseparable from them. Let us be content with blessing the philosophy and the humanity that have now joined forces to promise us wise institutions which will lead to equalizing wealth, raising the wages for work and insuring its just reward, and offering to all classes of society, and especially to the poor, more enjoyment and happiness."

Now we must return to 1783.

In his experiments on respiration, as in his others, Lavoisier did not base his research on the accepted theory of phlogiston; but neither did he come to grips with it. He only pointed out—on many occasions—that his theory of burning better fitted the facts.

Few of his contemporaries were ready to reject the idea of phlogiston, even after Lavoisier had showed up its weaknesses. Most of the older chemists defended the theory developed by the Germans—Johann Joachim Becher and Georg Ernst Stahl—during the previous century. Among them were some of the most prominent scientists: Priestley and Cavendish in England, Macquer in France (who thought that light had weight, even if fire and heat were weightless), and Benjamin Franklin. Although he spent a great deal of time in the Lavoisiers' home, and after leaving France corresponded with them warmly,

Franklin was fully as intimate with Priestley, to whom he wrote in 1773: "I shall like to hear how M. Lavoisier's Doctrine supports itself as I suppose it will be controverted."

When Franklin came to Paris in 1776 to negotiate for money and gunpowder for the Continental Army, he observed many experiments at the Arsenal and attended meetings of the Academy. As late as in 1782 he again wrote to Priestley: "Yesterday the Count du Nord * was at the Academy of Sciences, when sundry Experiments were exhibited for his entertainment: among them, one by M. Lavoisier, to show that the strongest fire we yet know, is made in a Charcoal blown upon with dephlogisticated air. In a Heat so produced, he melted Platina [crude platinum] presently, the fire being much more powerful than that of the strongest burning mirror." (Note that Franklin still uses the term "dephlogisticated air," three years after Lavoisier gave it the name oxygen.)

In reply, Priestley wrote Franklin: ". . . . my experiments are certainly inconsistent with Mr. Lavoisier's supposition, of there being no such thing as phlogiston, . . . I explain Mr. Lavoisier's experiments by supposing that precipitate per se contains all the phlogiston of the mercury, but in a different state; but I can show other calces which also contain more phlogiston than the metals themselves."

Not until 1783, after more than a decade of experimentation, was Lavoisier ready to denounce the theory which he believed had been completely disproved by the facts of chemistry. In a report read before the Academy, called

* The future Tsar Paul I of Russia, who was traveling incognito.

"Reflections on Phlogiston," he pointed out its weaknesses, one by one:

> "If phlogiston, the matter of heat and light, escapes through the walls of a sealed vessel, and by the most sensitive scale it cannot be shown that there was a loss in weight, then this escaped phlogiston must be weightless.
>
> "But if charcoal, on burning, yields fixed air weighing as much as the charcoal and the oxygen together, and fixed air cannot escape, is then phlogiston a substance with weight? Can the same substance possess weight and be weightless?
>
> "Sometimes it has weight, sometimes it has not; sometimes it is free fire, sometimes it is fire combined with earth; sometimes it passes through pores of vessels, sometimes these are impenetrable to it . . .
>
> "It is time to lead chemistry back to a stricter way of thinking, to strip the facts, with which this science is daily enriched, of the additions of rationality and prejudice, to distinguish what is fact and observation from what is system and hypothesis."

With these fiery words backed by dozens of facts, Lavoisier finally dared (in 1783), openly to challenge the phlogiston theory.

# 12. NOT PHLOGISTON, NOT ACID—BUT WATER

*The morning* after he had read his paper on phlogiston before the Academy, Lavoisier and his wife were chatting over their late breakfast. It was ten o'clock and Antoine had, as usual, already put in almost four hours' work in his laboratory. The rest of the day would be given to his duties in connection with the Tax-Farm and the many committees on which he served; in the evening, he would spend another three hours in his laboratory. This was one of the rare mornings when Madame Lavoisier had not assisted her husband in the laboratory adjoining their living quarters in the Arsenal. But she knew, of course, that Antoine had reported the results of the experiments on animal heat to the Academy. What was on his mind now?

"What do you think they will say of my paper?" he asked, as if expecting only one answer.

"It's hard to see how anyone would not have been persuaded by the logic of your theory. The title should have been 'Challenge to,' instead of 'Reflections on' phlogiston," she said.

"Fourcroy still sticks to his guns," Antoine replied.

"But most of the younger men are enthusiastic. To their fresh minds it all seems so clear," Madame Lavoisier assured him.

"But in England? Will it convince old Cavendish and Priestley? Will they give up their outworn theory?"

"That will come, too, Antoine; the facts are on your side."

"But the chemists aren't—except for Black, of course. Is it only prejudice that stands in their way now, or is there still a piece missing in the puzzle?"

He continued to muse aloud. "The mystery of burning is solved. A combustible body can burn, give off flame and light, only when it is in contact with oxygen. Plunge a burning body into a vacuum or into a vessel with fixed air, and it is extinguished as if it had been plunged into water.

"In every combustion there is an increase in the weight of the body burned—"

"Yes," Marie continued for him, "and the increase is exactly equal to the air it absorbs. You proved it with the precision balance, the most delicate balance in all of Europe."

And nowhere did phogiston fit into the proof!

Then why did Fourcroy and Macquer fail to see the contradictions in their phlogiston theory? Sometimes phlogiston had weight and at other times it was weightless.

How could one and the same substance be the weightless matter of fire and light, and the ponderable matter of charcoal? Was it only the conservatism of his colleagues, or were there still some unsolved problems which stood in the way of his gaining more supporters for his theory?

Madame Lavoisier recalled to him the words of his own report:

> "I do not expect that my ideas will be adopted at once; the human mind inclines to one way of thinking and those who have looked at Nature from a certain point of view during a part of their lives adopt new ideas only with difficulty; it is for time, therefore, to confirm or reject the opinions that I have advanced."

Still Lavoisier was troubled. He was not even satisfied with his own words, for he had not answered the question: what happens to "inflammable air" (hydrogen), and what is formed when, on burning, it combines with oxygen?

Then, as if suddenly remembering something, he pulled out a letter from Finance Minister d'Ormesson. He read aloud from it: "You have long known my views. I take this opportunity of affording you proof of them by informing the Farm of my wish that you should be appointed to the Committee of Administration. I believe that they will readily acquiesce in my wishes, as I am well aware of the respect and consideration in which you are held by them."

On hearing this, Marie Lavoisier may have been pleased, but hardly surprised. After all, her husband had served on so many committees; he had been entrusted with the direction of the import duties for Paris, with the accounts of the salt works, with the control of tobacco sales, and now the Committee on Administration of the Tax-Farm. But committees or no committees, she knew that until it was answered, he would come back again and again to the question of burning hydrogen.

When he did find the answer, he was to give the death blow to the phlogiston theory and complete the chemical revolution born out of his rediscovery and naming of oxygen. And, as happened so often, his work was an extension and reinterpretation of that by another scientist, Henry Cavendish.

The son of an English nobleman, Henry Cavendish was one of the richest men in England. But he had no use for his inherited wealth, living as a recluse, never owning more than one suit at a time, and caring neither for his appearance nor his health. People called him queer, for he was neither jealous nor ambitious, and cared not at all for honor or praise from his contemporaries. He had just one consuming interest—probing the secrets of Nature. With an apparatus he had devised—an improvement on Stephen Hales' pneumatic trough—he isolated, in 1766, the gas we now call hydrogen.

He threw some bits of zinc into a flask containing sulphuric acid, sealed the mouth of the flask with a cork through which he passed a glass tube, and connected the other end of the tube to a bladder. At first slowly, then rapidly, bubbles of a colorless gas began to rise in the tube, and pass into the bladder. When the bladder was full, Cavendish sealed it off and set it aside.

He repeated the experiment using other metals—tin and iron. Moreover, with each metal, he used hydrochloric instead of sulphuric acid. Each time he collected another bladder full of gas, until he had a row of six samples obtained from two acids and three different metals.

Next he touched a lighted taper to the mouth of the bladders, and the gas in each one burned with a pale blue flame. What could this "inflammable air" be? Was it phlogiston? After all, most people believed that metals were compounds of phlogiston and some peculiar earth. Cavendish himself was certain that the gas had not come from either the acid or the water, but from the *metals.*

To free it of all moisture, he then passed the gas through drying tubes and weighed it. It was very light, but still it had weight. Cavendish couldn't be sure whether or not he had isolated phlogiston or the "principle of fire." More important, he did not realize that he had discovered the colorless gas, hydrogen.

In 1776, Pierre Joseph Macquer set fire to this gas in ordinary air, and noted that as the gas burned, droplets of a colorless liquid formed on a porcelain saucer he held in the flame. What was the colorless liquid?

The next year Lavoisier was experimenting with this "inflammable air," and the same question arose in his mind: What formed when the gas burned? Was it "fixed air," as in other combustions? Repeating the experiment over limewater, Lavoisier found that the liquid did not turn milky, so it could not be "fixed air." Nor was an acid formed as Lavoisier had expected. He was so firmly convinced that oxygen was an acid-former that he expected to find it in the burning of inflammable air. The problem remained unsolved.

Four years later, in 1781, using an electric spark to explode a mixture of hydrogen with ordinary air inside a closed vessel, Joseph Priestley noticed that the inside of the vessel became covered with "dew." Priestley told Cavendish about the "dew" he had noticed, whereupon Cavendish set out to confirm the experiment. He, too, found that moisture formed inside the glass globes in which he exploded mixtures of the inflammable gas and air. He also found that he could reduce the volume of air by one fifth, and no more, and concluded that the inflammable air and the common air condensed in the "dew." But he failed to understand that the two "airs" had *combined* to form the *new* substance of the "dew."

Going further, he used the newly discovered oxygen instead of common air. Now the gas burned until it was completely used up, and many a flask was broken when it exploded. But the weighings and measurings still had to be done, and Cavendish was not one to hurry an experiment, to jump to conclusions in order to rush his results into print. At long last, however, he said, ". . . by this experiment it appears that this dew is plain water." The "airs" had condensed into "plain water," but *still* Cavendish missed seeing that there was a chemical combination between them. Instead, he explained the formation of water in this way: "Water consists of dephlogisticated air united with phlogiston." (By "dephlogisticated air" he meant water deprived of its phlogiston.) The condensation that occurred when the mixture was exploded was explained by Cavendish as the formation of water from *each* of the "airs" (dephlogisticated and inflammable).

Blinded, like so many others, by the phlogiston theory, he could not foresee the necessary last step in his experiment, and so Cavendish failed to realize that he had discovered the composition of water!

Henry Cavendish never sought publicity; his only interest was experimentation. He sent no sealed notes to the Royal Society and, unlike Lavoisier, he did not try to insure his getting credit for a discovery. He even delayed publication of his results until they had been verified and verified again, but he did speak of his experiments to his scientist friends. Long before he presented his paper to the Royal Society, many knew about his work.

The continuation of this story leads us back to Lavoisier's laboratory, leaving Cavendish to his further study of "airs."

In the summer of 1783, the Lavoisiers had another visitor from England. But this occasion turned out to be different from the usual call of a foreign scientist, for Charles Blagden had worked with Cavendish on the hydrogen-burning experiments.

Impressed with Cavendish's observations, Blagden described to Lavoisier and Marie the explosions resulting from the combination of hydrogen with oxygen, and the formation of "dew" in the vessels. The Lavoisiers listened with more than their usual eagerness. No doubt their recent conversation on the theory of burning was still fresh in their minds.

"Did inflammable air really yield water when it burned?" Lavoisier wanted to know.

"Yes, there were droplets of pure water," Blagden asserted.

"It burned in oxygen, and still there was no acid formed?" asked Antoine, firm in his belief that oxygen was an acid-former. But Cavendish's observation was important; the experiment needed to be repeated, the results confirmed, and Lavoisier lost no time in doing it.

With the help of Laplace, he immediately set to work while Blagden looked on and Madame Lavoisier took notes. On the very next day (June 25, 1783) Lavoisier sent a brief report to the Academy, stating that when inflammable air burned in ordinary air, in a closed vessel, the result was "water in a very pure state."

By the autumn of that year Cavendish had published nothing, but Lavoisier was ready to make his discovery known to the scientific world. On November 12th, he proclaimed to his fellow Academicians that water was not an element, since it could be "decomposed and recombined." Sure of his facts and confident of his interpretation, Lavoisier went on to describe the experiments.

He and Laplace had burned measured volumes of the two gases over mercury inside a glass receiver. Droplets of water formed on the walls of the glass and drained onto the mercury, from which it was collected. It weighed nearly as much as the combined weights of the two gases. So water was composed of inflammable air and oxygen. It was not an element—as had been thought until then—but a compound of the two gases we now call hydrogen and oxygen.

Though Lavoisier's hurried experiments did not yield the accurate results of Cavendish's painstaking work, it was his conclusion that was important. While Cavendish showed that the burning of inflammable gas yielded water, Lavoisier, for the first time, recognized that water was the *chemical combination of two known gases.* With his characteristic genius, he saw the last step in a long chain of previous discoveries.

Later, to add proof upon proof, Lavoisier not only compounded water from its elements but also broke it down into its component parts. In a vessel containing mercury he placed a small amount of water and some unrusted iron filings and inverted the container over another dish which held mercury. Gradually, with the oxygen from the water, the iron filings rusted, setting free a small amount of inflammable air. The rusted iron gained in weight by just the amount of oxygen it absorbed, while the weight of the hydrogen was determined from the volume accumulated at the top of the mercury. It all checked. Water had been broken down into its two elements which, on recombining, would form water once more.

The composition of water had been established, but now a new controversy arose. When Lavoisier presented his report to the Academy, he made only slight reference to the work of Cavendish, giving the impression that it confirmed his own. Cavendish, though he had completed his experiment before Lavoisier had begun his, did not read his paper to the Royal Society of England until the following year. Charles Blagden felt it was his duty to insert a note saying that he had informed Lavoisier of Cavendish's experiments on his visit to Paris in 1783. He accused Lavoisier of having "really discovered nothing but what had been pointed out to him to have been previously made out and demonstrated in England."

These were strong words, and the same reproach had been made before on the occasion of the discovery of oxygen. When Lavoisier at that time was accused of borrowing the work of others, he replied, "It will at least not be disputed that the conclusions are my own."

For many years a bitter controversy about who had discovered the composition of water raged between the admirers of Lavoisier and the defenders of Cavendish.

Actually, as is not always true in such arguments, the contribution of each man stands out clearly: Cavendish had priority in obtaining the results; Lavoisier gave the correct explanation of the same results. Lavoisier sometimes did fail to acknowledge the contributions of those who came before him; this did not, however, detract from his scientific integrity.

Lavoisier's discovery of the composition of water removed the last stumbling block to the acceptance of the new theory of the role of oxygen in oxidation. Before this revolutionary discovery, the conversion of metals into their calces, or rust, had been explained by everyone in the same terms that Cavendish used ("their phlogiston flies off"), and even Lavoisier's theory could not provide a complete explanation because the part played by water was not understood. Now it all became clear: The hydrogen had come from the water, and the oxygen thus liberated converted the metal into its calx (oxide).

There was no phlogiston in this reaction. The phlogiston theory was no longer needed to explain either oxidation or the evolution of hydrogen. The problem was explained by the discovery of the composition of water, and soon chemists everywhere began to accept the new theory of oxidation.

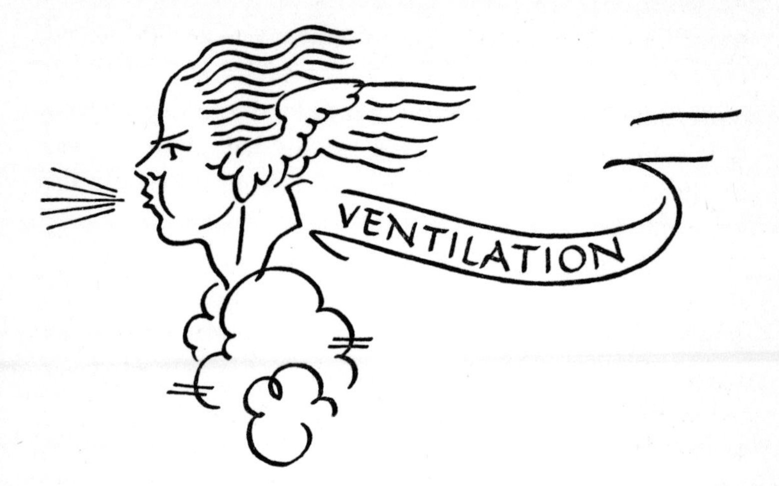


## 13. THE REFORMER

*Lavoisier* had joined the Tax-Farm in 1768. He went in as assistant, buying one-third of a share for 500,000 livres. In 1771, by paying an additional 260,000 livres, he increased his holdings to a half share, and in 1779, when one of his associates died, Lavoisier bought an additional half share, becoming a full Farmer-General. At the same time the office of assistant was abolished, and the total number of Farm members was reduced from sixty to forty. This was intended as a reform measure, to exclude men who bought into the Farm and drew fat profits, but contributed no services. The shares of these inactive members with partial membership were distributed among the remaining full members, and the interest rate was set at 7 per cent of their investment, which meant that each Farmer-General received 75,000 livres a year, with an additional 32,000 livres for expenses. As one of the forty, Lavoisier annually drew from the Farm an income that would be considered high today, even for the president of a large corporation.

Because of his diligence and exceptional administrative ability, Lavoisier was appointed to one Farm committee after another. Entrusted first with the collection of import duties of Paris, then with those of the salt and tobacco taxes in several districts, he was finally chosen also for the Farm's most important post, the Committee on Administration. In all of these posts, much like an executive in a modern business firm, he introduced changes to make the organization work more efficiently. He also tried to distribute the taxes more fairly.

One of his proposals was to equalize the customs duties at all boundaries of the various provinces of France. This, he maintained, would not only cut down by thousands the number of customs officials, but would decrease the smuggling that resulted from the inequality of taxes. Because of the provincial differences in the rate of the *gabelle,* for instance, the cost of salt was twenty to thirty times higher in one province than in another. As a result, where the tax was high the people bought salt from smugglers (who brought it in from other provinces) instead of from the government. Many petty officials of the Farm saw it as their duty to enter private homes in search of smuggled salt. Naturally, this didn't increase the organization's popularity; the people came to hate its members as a band of unscrupulous fleecers. When the government put the death penalty on salt smuggling, the searches were intensified.

When Turgot became Controller General of Finances,

he determined to clear France of these abuses. For this purpose, he chose Lavoisier to improve the workings of the Farm, to equalize taxes, and at the same time to bring more money into the treasury. But Lavoisier's proposed reforms were criticized and angrily rejected by the people. Smugglers were bringing merchandise into Paris illegally, to sell to those who wished to avoid import duties. A cry went up from the tradesmen who *were* paying the duty. This increased the price of their goods over that of their competitors who were buying smuggled goods. Lavoisier proposed the construction of a wall around Paris to prevent the entrance of smuggled goods. The architect who drew up the plans made them so elaborate that when the wall was built it cost 30,000,000 livres. The citizens of Paris resented it not only as an extravagance, but as a restriction on their freedom. Some even said that the Tax-Farm was trying to cut off the fresh air from Paris and to prevent the escape of the foul air which pervaded the insanitary city. They expressed their resentment in verses and street songs directed at Lavoisier, whom they already mistrusted because of his wealth, because he had originated the idea of the wall.

There was a tragic side to the efforts of Antoine Lavoisier and other leaders to reform the deplorable conditions in eighteenth-century France. They were trying to patch up a decrepit and dying system that was doomed. But Lavoisier, the great theorist, brilliant experimenter, and creative chemist, continued to apply what he had learned in his laboratory to everyday problems, always with the hope of improving the living conditions of his countrymen. In his boyhood, he had been disturbed by the misery he saw in the streets of Paris; in his travels as a young scientist, studying the physical resources of France, he had been depressed by the peasants' poverty and backbreaking toil. His work for the Tax-Farm led him to sympathize even more with the underprivileged majority. When he was in charge of the Farm's administration for the district of Clermontois, he had succeeded in having abolished a special tax that was paid by Jews, the *pied fourchu*, or cloven hoof. In gratitude, the Jewish congregation of Metz sent a deputation to thank him.

As Lavoisier's interest in the sources and analysis of water inspired his attempt to improve the water supply of Paris, so did his work on combustion and respiration lead him to the study of ventilation. Shortly after his work with Laplace on body heat, Lavoisier read a paper before the Royal Society of Medicine in which he set forth his ideas on the ventilation of crowded rooms. Noting that animals showed discomfort after rebreathing the same air, he attributed this to decreased oxygen and increased carbon dioxide in the air: in breathing, the "eminently respirable" air, containing oxygen, was used up, while the "mephitic" part (nitrogen) remained inactive and unchanged. At the same time, oxygen was converted into carbon dioxide.

He was wrong in attributing the discomfort of people in crowded rooms solely to the *chemical* changes in ordinary air, for animal heat, moisture, and odors are chiefly responsible for the effects of poor ventilation. In his day, these causes were not yet understood, but his observations of their effects were correct. He remarked that toward the end of a meeting of the Academy the members became fidgety and inattentive, a distinct disadvantage to the one who happened to be the last speaker on the program.

In January 1780, the Academy of Sciences appointed a

commission to report on a plan for new prisons. Lavoisier was a member of this commission, too, and, as almost always happened, he drew up the report which may still be read in his handwriting.

Prisons are not inviting places anywhere or at any time, but those of Europe in the eighteenth century, with the possible exception of Germany and Holland, would be considered intolerable today. Conditions in the three Paris prisons studied by the commission—the large and small Chatelet and Fort-l'Evêque—were unbelievably bad. As many as 1,000 prisoners were kept in a total area of about 3,500 square feet, giving each prisoner less than four square feet of floor space, barely enough room to stand or sit in; it is hard to know how they could have slept. The prison walls were so high and the ceilings of the cells so low that hardly any daylight reached the prisoners' quarters. Their clothes rotted on their backs, and the straw they slept on was vermin-infested and decayed. Privies opened into the cells, their stench and "infectious vapors" poisoning the air.

The Academy report included several badly needed recommendations for more humane treatment: Debtors and other civil offenders were to be separated from criminals, the women from the men, and the sick from the healthy. The old structures were to be demolished and new prisons built, with facilities for maintaining cleanliness, including plenty of water for washing and drinking; air was to circulate freely, and food was to be adequate. An underground tunnel would carry away sewage, and there would be vents to draw off the odors.

Lavoisier had a hand in designing floors with proper drainage, and an ample water supply to wash away the wastes and to clean the yards, cells, kitchens, and mess halls. Privies were to be removed from the cells, individual cots provided, prison clothing disinfected by heat and live steam, and the straw on the cots renewed frequently. No detail for minimum human comfort and decency was omitted. Three years later, an English visitor examined the new prisons and found them much better than those in England.

Even more shocking than the conditions in the Parisian prisons were those in its main hospital, the Hôtel-Dieu. Again Lavoisier was one of eight commissioners appointed to recommend needed reforms. They found 2,000 patients in the hospital, and only 1,200 beds; sometimes as many as six patients occupied one bed, while others lay on an overhanging canopy. Corpses were mixed with the living, the contagious patients with the noncontagious, the insane with the sane. Filth, vermin, pollution, and foul air were everywhere. In this atmosphere mothers delivered babies, their cries mingling with those of the surgical, the feverish, and the insane patients. The hospital was itself a breeder of ill health, epidemics, unspeakable misery, and death.

In 1785, the Royal Society of Medicine made its hospital recommendations on the basis of Lavoisier's studies on respiration:

Each person was to have a minimum of 5 cubic feet of air an hour.

The amount of air required by each patient varied with the nature of the disease. People suffering from smallpox, scurvy, insanity, high fevers, and infections needed high ceilings to provide more air. Those with hay fever, asthma, internal diseases, and the debilities of old age required less.

Buildings of more than three stories were condemned, because the sickening air accumulated in the upper floors, producing headaches and difficult breathing. The bad air, Lavoisier pointed out, was lighter, and hence rose to the upper floors, taking with it all sorts of disease-carrying "vapors," or what we would call today air-borne organisms.

Two members of the commission had gone to England to bring back proposals for the construction of new hospital buildings. Included in the Society's recommendations were details of water supply, ventilation, and sewage disposal, not very different from what is required in a hospital today.

The King ordered four new hospitals to be constructed according to the commission's plans. But the storm clouds of the coming Revolution were gathering, and the plans for the buildings were abandoned. Lavoisier's work, however, was not altogether in vain, for the Glasgow Infirmary, in Scotland, was constructed with "every part . . . as much as possible, according to a report to the late king of France, by a committee of the Academy." The report was signed, among others, by Lavoisier.

In 1787, Lavoisier was elected as representative of the Third Estate from Romorantin, a small town near his estate at Fréchines, to the Provincial Assembly of Orléanais. On September 5th, accompanied by Madame Lavoisier, he attended the opening meeting in Orléans. The assembly was in session for about three months, and Antoine was obliged to be absent on Tax-Farm business several times. However, he once more demonstrated his amazing capacity for organization and work in the meetings he attended. The assembly was meeting to consider reforms in the governorship of the province, and many other matters were involved in the consideration of the subject. Always eager to advance his ideas for improving existing social conditions, Lavoisier was an effective speaker in this gathering. He proposed reforms in the *corvée,* or forced labor by peasants on the roads; the establishment of charity workshops, to give employment to the poor and disabled, and a savings bank.

Especially interesting to us was his proposal for a scheme of insurance for the aged. He opened his report by saying: "Happy is he who, surrounded by a grateful and tender family, receives from them in his last years the help that he lavished on them in the vigor of his younger days, and who is led to the end of his life through a quiet and tranquil old age. But such happiness in the last years of life is not given to all men."

He went on to point out that many workingmen made scarcely enough to support their wives and children, and could not provide for their aged parents. "We are not unaware that hearts that are unmoved at the sight of suffering humanity look upon an old man, condemned by feebleness to idleness, as a burden to society which it is to the common interest to be rid of," he declared, "and that they will be little touched by the care that we are taking to obtain support for this class of unfortunates. It is not to those hard hearts that we are addressing ourselves. The burning zeal that animates you for the well-being of humanity, the spirit of patriotism with which you are penetrated, reply in advance that there are none such among you."

According to Lavoisier's plan, workers wishing to insure themselves and their dependents could deposit money in a savings bank, thus assuring themselves of an annuity in later years. The program was to be organized in a business-like manner, and the province was to be the guarantor of the commitments undertaken by the bank. His plan anticipated the modern organization of contributory state insurance or social security.

Lavoisier was nominated to be one of six members of the assembly to serve on an intermediary commission which continued to meet until 1790. Unfortunately, the Provincial Assembly of Orléanais never convened again, and none of the reforms it advocated was ever accomplished.

The genius of Antoine Lavoisier is also seen in his brilliant application of the scientific knowledge of his day to industrial hygiene: better conditions for miners; the prevention of adulteration of foods, of spoilage of grain and flour; better methods for purifying sugar; the control of hazards from fumes in hat-making, and the dangers of using certain metals in cooking utensils. In all instances, to correct the injustices that beset the poor and to improve the health of the people, he made use of his wide knowledge of climate, air movements, water supply, nutrition, and chemistry.

As a seeker of knowledge and a social reformer, Lavoisier was the undisputed pioneer of many innovations which are of benefit to human beings the world over. Many of his reforms and contributions to the bettering of living conditions were so sound that they have not been much improved upon even today.

# 14. SCIENTIFIC FARMING

*In addition* to being the founder of modern chemistry and a pioneer in the fields of respiration and human nutrition, Lavoisier was also the first to undertake experimental farming. He had inherited a house in the country at Le Bourget, while his family had their country home in Villet-Cotterets, where he and Madame Lavoisier spent their vacations. But these did not suit the purpose of his venture into farming. Early in his married life he bought an estate and a magnificent chateau at Fréchines, in the parish of Ville-Francoeur, halfway between Blois and Vendôme. Here he applied himself for ten years (1778–1788) to the practical problems of agriculture, with the same skill and mastery he was known for in his laboratory experiments.

In 1788 he was invited to make a report to the Royal

Society of Agriculture in Paris. In this report, Lavoisier recalled that at the time he began his work in Fréchines, the wheat yield was only five times the amount of seed planted. He asked himself if this was due to the poverty of the soil or to improper cultivation. To answer his own question, he began to observe the agricultural conditions in this area. He found that the small herds of cows and flocks of sheep each farmer owned were not enough to provide fertilizer for the land on which they grazed, and because the land was poorly manured, the pastures were thin and the fodder meager. This, in turn, meant less food for the animals, and again too little manure to produce lush fields of hay.

Lavoisier pondered over the problem of how to make the land more productive. If, instead of being permitted to roam, sheep were confined to a small, enclosed field, wouldn't they have enough to eat and at the same time furnish enough manure to enrich the restricted area? Then if the sheep were moved to another fenced-in area, wouldn't the hay have a chance to grow abundantly in the first one? He reasoned that by thus successively rotating grazing and hay-growing, the land would be enriched, and would provide *more* food for *more* stock. This simple practice of modern farming was not being used—indeed, it had never been heard of—by the farmers in Lavoisier's neighborhood at Fréchines. But he was determined, by using proper husbandry on his own estate, to help his farmer-neighbors.

Lavoisier didn't have all the answers at first—these would require experimentation. So he selected 240 acres of his poorest soil and, for comparison, took half-shares in three adjacent farms where the land gave a better yield.

His experiments taught him a great deal about which crops prospered in a given area, and which did poorly. For example, alfalfa did not grow on his land because of the presence of a plant parasite, but a good crop of sainfoin could be obtained. Clover grew well in wet years, but failed in dry years. Potatoes and turnips flourished in open fields; peas and beans did better on restricted, fallow land. After several years, he had enough facts and figures—for he kept accurate records of his farming, even weighing the various crops each year—to convince even the most doubting farmer.

But Lavoisier was no idle dreamer or ivory-tower theorist, and he soon realized that what he had been able to accomplish depended only partly on sound farming practices. For one thing, there had to be enough money available to buy more stock, because the process of enriching the land was slow and money invested would not yield a return for several years. The average farmer could not afford to make the needed long-term investment that was easy for Lavoisier, the rich landowner. And if a farmer *were* prosperous he could get larger and quicker returns if he invested his money in public loans, on which the interest rate was high. So Lavoisier maintained that the national prosperity demanded that the government reduce the interest rate on loans.

But, supposing that a farmer was persuaded to make the investment in new stock, and to let some of his land lie fallow, there still was another obstacle to his benefiting from scientific farming. This was the *taille*, or property tax, which increased with the number of horses and cattle the farmer owned. The best stocked farms paid the highest tax, and so the industrious and intelligent farmer was penalized for his efforts to improve his land. Lavoisier made the obviously important recommendation: The tax system had to be changed!

He went even further, instituting a system of accounting by which he plainly showed what happened to the earnings of a peasant who did not own his own farm. Of the income from the crop, so much went to pay for harvesting, so much for threshing, so much for land that was reserved for next year's sowing; this much was needed for the upkeep of the farm, the equipment, and the buying of more stock; still more was needed for rent to the owner of the land and for all the various taxes. (The landowner claimed one-third of the harvest, and the taxes took almost as much.) What was left for the farmer and his family?

Moreover, if the land produced well, the rental went up since the leases were short and rent was based on the past performance of the farm. If, after applying Lavoisier's methods for five or more years, the peasant had enriched the land and increased its yield, a new lease required his paying more rent. To remedy this situation, Lavoisier advocated a twenty-seven-year lease, so the farmer could benefit from his industry and long-term investment. This reform was also being introduced in England and Flanders.

Lavoisier's economic proposals, were based on the theories of the *physiocrats*, an important group of *philosophes*, who believed that the most important source of a nation's wealth is land. It was logical, therefore, that he would follow Turgot, Du Pont de Nemours, Quesnay, and other leading physiocrats, in calling for a minimum of restrictions on farm property. If it were unhampered by oppressive taxation, short leases, and high interest rates, agriculture would flourish, and benefit the nation as well as the peasants. A similar policy of unrestricted trade and commerce was also considered essential to the nation's prosperity. These views, of course, reflected the needs of the richer section of the Third Estate—the merchants, traders, wealthy farmers, and manufacturers—the group of which Lavoisier was a member.

His interest in and original contributions to agriculture led to his election in 1783 to the Society of Agriculture, an organization that became so important it later received from the King the title of *Royal* Society. It gained renown in other countries as well as France, and regular correspondence was carried on with Benjamin Franklin and George Washington, the Duke of Parma in Italy, and Arthur Young and Sir Joseph Banks in England.

At this time a Committee of Agriculture was also appointed by the Court, and once more Lavoisier was selected to act as secretary, a position which often ended with his not only writing the reports but gathering much of the material for them.

One of his first proposals was that agricultural stations for carrying out experiments of the kind he had initiated be set up near Paris. (Today these experimental stations are to be found in all scientifically advanced countries.) For this purpose he offered the Committee the use of his property at Le Bourget.

Another of his proposals, one that was adopted, was for the establishment of schools to train people in the skills of weaving. There was a logical reason for this. France grew large crops of flax and hemp, but it exported these raw materials for manufacture. As a result, Frenchmen had to pay high prices for imported linen, rope, and other products manufactured abroad from its own crops.

Since the nearly bankrupt government could not finance the schools, the Committee itself established them with privately contributed funds, and France entered into the manufacture of linen. In a very short time Lavoisier had improved this process too, by using chlorine in the commercial bleaching of cloth, a process introduced by Berthollet.

If only a few of the ideas born in Lavoisier's fertile brain had been permitted to become practical facts, France would have seen many important agricultural reforms: the establishment of model farms, government subsidies for the distribution of seed, a twofold increase in yield per acre, more cattle, more fodder, improved methods of farming, and the elimination of wasteful methods, with more land under cultivation. But most of his ingenious plans never materialized, for they fell on the deaf or indifferent ears of a corrupt government that saw no need for improving the conditions of its people.

Lacking financial support, the Committee of Agriculture was disbanded in 1787, two years before the Revolution.

# 15. THE NEW CHEMISTRY

*While Lavoisier* was busying himself with matters of state, traveling between Paris and Fréchines, receiving and studying reports of plantings and harvests, attending meetings and making proposals on questions of ventilation and sanitation for hospitals, theaters, and prisons, he did not neglect his laboratory work in chemistry. With his customary energy, skill, insight, and logic, he was working on a revision of the outmoded and chaotic method of naming chemicals.

Up to this time there had been no system of chemical nomenclature. There was only a confused jumble of names inherited from the alchemists. Some chemicals were named for their discoverers, others for their resemblance to something familiar, one for the place where it was found, another for a planet it was supposed to be associated with. *Nordhausen oil of vitriol* was sulphuric acid, *black vitriol* was impure copper sulphate; *vitriol of Venus* was copper sulphate, *oxidized muriatic acid* was chlorine; *calx* of a metal was its oxide, and *Epsom salt* (from the mineral springs in Epsom, Surrey, England), was magnesium sulphate. Some had many names: there were sixteen different ones for lead, and thirty-five for mercury!

Lavoisier soon realized that the confusion of alchemical terminology had to be swept away along with the phlogiston theory. The new chemistry required an up-to-date nomenclature based on an organized system. He was not alone in this idea; in fact, someone else already had come to grips with the problem of names. Guyton de Morveau, while editing the chemical sections of the *Encyclopédie*, found it difficult to make sense with the old nomenclature. He proposed the creation of a new and meaningful system, but the phlogistonists saw no reason for it; they considered such a change to be high treason against their chemical ancestors.

De Morveau came to Paris to defend his views, and there he found firm supporters in Antoine François Fourcroy, Claude-Louis Berthollet, and Lavoisier. Fourcroy and Berthollet had accepted the new chemistry and readily saw the need for a sensible terminology. The four men met frequently in Lavoisier's laboratory, and together they went to work on the gigantic task of creating a new language of chemistry.

Lavoisier argued with his usual boldness of conviction: "We must clean house thoroughly, for they have made use of an enigmatic language, which was peculiar to themselves, which most frequently had one meaning for the initiated and another for the novice, and which had nothing exact or intelligible for either the one or the other. . . . It is now time to rid chemistry of every kind of impediment that delays its advance; to introduce into it a true spirit of analysis. . . . The names that are now in use, such as those of powder of algaroth, salt of alembroth, pompholix, phagadenic water, turbith mineral, colcothar, and many others, are neither less harsh nor less extraordinary [than the new terms]. The names of oil of tartar per deliquium, oil of vitriol, butter of arsenic, flowers of zinc, are still more ridiculous, because they give rise to false ideas. . . . There does not exist in the mineral kingdom, and especially among the metals, either butter or oil or flowers . . . the substances designated by these deceitful names are for the most part violent poisons."

In the new system, the substances to be named first were those which the four men considered "not decomposed," and therefore "simple." There were fifty-five in this list, roughly corresponding to the modern chemical elements. The names were derived from the Greek and expressed some well-known properties of characteristics of the substances. Thus the term *hydrogen*, from the words "water" and "originating," indicated that it was one of the constituents of water. *Oxygen* meant "giving rise to acid" (an incorrect belief of Lavoisier's). Heat and light were included, incorrectly, in the list of "substances."

The second group contained the principal elements of the common acids: *phosphorus*, *sulphur*, *carbon*, and *azote* (meaning not living and later changed to *nitrogen*).

The third group contained the metals: mercury, silver, iron, tin, lead, copper, platinum, antimony, manganese, nickel, cobalt, arsenic, bismuth, gold, and tungsten. For the first time, these were classified as simple, "undecomposed" substances (according to the phlogiston theory they were compounds), and the correctness of the new chemistry was reflected in the grouping together of all metals.

The next group ("simple earthy substances") contained lime, magnesia, alumina, and silica.

Another group was made up of the compounds we now call the alkalies or bases, such as soda, potash, and ammonia.

Then came compounds, composed of two or more simple substances, which included the acids, composed of oxygen ("the acidifying principle" as Lavoisier thought), and one other element from which they got their names. There were nitric acid containing nitrogen, and nitrous acid containing less oxygen and the same amount of nitrogen. There were sulphric and sulphurous acid, phosphoric and carbonic acid.

Their *salts* were, in turn, called nitrates and nitrites, sulphates and sulphites, phosphates and carbonates.

Instead of calces, there were now *oxides*, combinations of oxygen and a metal as lead oxide, mercury oxide, etc.

In 1787, the new nomenclature was presented by de Morveau to the Academy. To those Academicians and chemists who had no axe to grind, the simplicity and logic of the system had great appeal. The rest gradually accepted it, but some skeptics continued to ridicule the new names. One English chemist was supposed to have sneered at the word *oxide*, saying it could not be distinguished from "the hide of an ox."

The four innovators prepared a table, arranged like a dictionary, with the old and new names side by side. It was promptly published under the name of *Méthode de Nomenclature Chimique.* Several editions appeared in French, others in English, German, Spanish, Italian, and Danish, and there were three editions in America.

This simple nomenclature, which has come down almost unchanged to our own day, is our great heritage from Lavoisier and his followers in the new and revolutionary science of chemistry.

Two years after publication of the *Nomenclature*, Lavoisier presented a complete and detailed account of the new chemistry in a volume called *Traité Elementaire de Chimie*, on whose foundation modern chemistry securely rests.

If a chemistry treatise or text could be said to be a best seller, the *Traité* certainly was that. One translation after another soon appeared. There was one in English by Robert Kerr, a member of the Royal College of Surgeons, under the title *Elements of Chemistry in a New Systematic Order, Containing All the Modern Discoveries.* It was illustrated with thirteen copper-plate drawings, painstakingly and accurately drawn and engraved by Madame Lavoisier. The original plates still exist, as well as her freehand sketches and water-color paintings of the apparatus. She had no graph paper to help her make her drawings in scale. After transferring the finished figures to the paper and then onto the copper plate, she wrote the word *Bonne* (good) and placed her initials on the final proof.

The *Traité* was organized into three parts. The first part dealt with the new system of chemistry, the second was devoted to acids, bases, and salts, while the third described the methods and apparatus used in the chemistry laboratory. It included a complete description of the analysis of air into its two principal gases—oxygen and nitrogen. The experiment is even today regarded as one of the most famous in the history of chemistry. According to the new nomenclature the word *gas* replaced *elastic fluid*, and the terms *oxygen* and *azote* (nitrogen) replaced "eminently respirable part of common air" and "mofette or irrespirable air," respectively. The proof that water is a compound of oxygen and hydrogen—as finally demonstrated by both analysis and resynthesis—was also furnished.

One section of the book dealt with the fermentation of fruit juices into carbonic acid and the "spirit of wine," now renamed from the original Arabic *alcohol*. For this reaction Lavoisier wrote the equation much as we would write it today:

$$\text{must of grapes} = \text{carbonic acid} + \text{alcohol}$$

"We must," he said, "consider the substances submitted to fermentation, and the products resulting from that operation, as forming an algebraic equation."

For the first time, too, he showed that the total weight of the final products in a reaction was equal to that of the materials originally present. In other words, the weight of each of the elements, before and after the chemical change, remained unchanged. *Nothing is created in the operations . . . an equal quantity of matter exists both before and after the operation.* This was Lavoisier's formulation, again for the first time, of the Law of Indestructibility of Matter, and the Law of the Conservation of Mass.

A list of elements was reproduced from the earlier nomenclature, and an element was defined as a "substance not decomposed—the simple and indivisible molecules that compose bodies." Concerning oil and salt, which had been regarded as elements, Lavoisier said, "Experiment and observation having brought new knowledge, it has since been shown that the salts are not simple but composed of an acid and a base, and that their neutrality results from this combination."

Lavoisier had intended the *Traité* to be an elementary text, but there were few mature chemists who were not beginners in the new science, so different was it from what had been taught before. He was now confident that the job he had begun twenty years earlier, to revolutionize the science, was complete. As he said: "All young chemists adopt the theory and from that I conclude that the revolution in chemistry has come to pass."

The revolution in chemistry had indeed come to pass. The struggle of a century's duration had ended with the world accepting the new ideas. There still were some diehards. Cavendish never surrendered his ideas of inflammable air, dephlogisticated air, and the "element" of water. Priestley, the dissenting preacher and fighter for human liberty, failed to see the dawn of a new day in chemistry. He remained to his dying day a conservative in chemistry, a confirmed phlogistonist.

# 16. THE FRENCH REVOLUTION

*At the pinnacle* of his triumph in one revolution, Lavoisier found himself immersed in another, the French Revolution, that was to free his country from the stranglehold of the old regime and cause his own death.

France was bankrupt. The treasury was hopelessly in debt, and the burden of taxes borne by the people could no longer be endured. The severe winter of 1788 and the crop failures brought more distress to all but the wealthy. People were beginning to denounce the oppressive taxation and injustices in every corner of the land. Meeting in the provinces, they drew up *cahiers de doléances*, or lists of grievances, and demanded that the King convene the Estates-General, the legislative and advisory body which had not met for 175 years. The kings of France and their nobles had ruled with absolute power since 1614. Faced with bankruptcy, Louis XVI agreed to summon the Estates-General, setting the date for May 5, 1789.

Every large city and bailiwick (electoral unit) in France accordingly elected representatives in proportion to its population and the taxes levied on it. When the Estates-General met at Versailles on May 5th, the clergy, or First Estate, had 308 representatives, the nobles, or Second Estate, 285, and the Third Estate, 621.

Nearly all of the Third Estate, as well as the more enlightened aristocrats and clergy, no longer believed that the King ruled by "divine right," or the will of God. However, they regarded him as indispensable to the state, and were sure that the reforms they proposed could be achieved with Louis XVI as the head of the government.

After weeks of debate on the method of voting, members of the Third Estate—joined by some of the nobles and clergy—set itself up as the National Assembly, and Bailly, a noted astronomer, was elected President.

The National Assembly was responsible to the people who had elected them, not to the King and the Court. Fearing the power of the Assembly, the King ordered their meeting place closed on June 17th, ostensibly to make repairs in the building.

The members of the Assembly declared their defiance of the King by holding their meeting on June 20, 1789, in another building, an indoor tennis court, where they took the historic "Oath of the Tennis Court," vowing "never to separate until the constitution of the realm is established and affirmed on a secure basis." Three days later, a messenger from the King ordered them to adjourn. Mirabeau, one of the noblemen who had joined the Assembly, answered for the rest. He cried: "Go and tell your master that we are here at the command of the people and we will disperse only at the point of the bayonet!" On June 27th, Louis XVI officially recognized the Assembly.

The King wavered between making concessions and breaking his promises, hoping that somehow he could strike a bargain with the National Assembly that would insure his position as head of the state, without a constitution. The Queen's Party, the Court faction most determined to maintain the absolute monarchy, regarded his policy as weak. Whether or not the King approved, they planned to disperse the Assembly, intimidate the people, get rid of their leaders where necessary, and re-establish the monarchy on the old basis.

To do this, they had to control Paris, and the town of Versailles, both of which had given full support to the Assembly. Therefore, the Queen's Party called on the Garde Française, one of the largest and best of the royal regiments, to disperse the crowds in Paris. However, the soldiers refused to fire on the people. The King's advisers then sent for mercenary troops from Switzerland and Germany. When word spread that the mercenaries were marching toward the capital, the people of Paris crowded the narrow streets, excited and angry. Among them were many beggars and criminals who hoped to plunder the disordered city. But there were also fiery patriots, earnest reformers, and orators, as well as many ordinary people, unemployed, hungry, and desperate.

The National Assembly sent a delegation to the King, protesting the concentration of troops and demanding the formation of their own guard to preserve order and protect the deputies. The King's reply was as blunt as it was ill-advised: If the deputies feared his troops, they could move their meeting place to a province far from the capital. Then on July 11th, he dismissed several of his ministers, including Necker, the popular Minister of Finance. It was now clear that Louis XVI had decided openly to challenge the deputies.

In the meantime, news of the revolt in Paris was the signal for uprisings in the countryside. Chateaux and convents were seized, and manors and tithe barns were looted. Records of landownership and peasants' indebtedness to their lords were burned. Families of the nobility fled across the borders and began to enlist the aid of foreigners who feared the spread of the revolution. It was said of southern England that during the summer of 1789 there were two great migrations: a swarm of French aristocrats fleeing the vengeance of the people they had oppressed, and another of game birds escaping from the French countryfolk, as the peasants were now hunting on the previously fenced-off preserves of the nobles.

Emigrés, gathered in Brussels, Coblenz, Worms, and Metz, set themselves up as a provisional government and started to collect forces for the invasion of France in a counterrevolution. Led by the Austrian Emperor, the brother of Marie Antoinette, all the kings on the Continent of Europe, prepared to invade France as soon as Louis XVI gave them the word. Meanwhile the nobles of the Court constituted a counterrevolutionary force within France, and were in constant touch with the emigrés and the Coalition of Kings.

The National Assembly had decided to organize the National Guard, a civil militia, to maintain order in Paris.

This militia was a volunteer force composed of people from all walks of life and from all the three estates—noblemen, merchants, financiers, even priests—and its ranks were swelled by many deserters from the King's mutinous regiments.

The militia needed arms and thought there were plenty in the Bastille, the infamous prison. Originally an ancient fortress outside the city walls, its towers now loomed high above the workingmen's section of Paris. Behind the prison's ten-foot-thick walls, deep in its medieval dungeons, were political prisoners condemned to end their days in darkness, torture, and unspeakable misery. For the people of France, and for freedom-loving people everywhere, the Bastille was a hated symbol of despotic oppression.

On July 14, 1789, when their petition for arms had been refused by the King, the people demonstrated in front of the Bastille. Their protests were met by gunfire, and more than a hundred civilians were killed. Enraged, the citizens of Paris stormed the fortress, liberated the prisoners, and took by force the arms they had been denied.

The King conceded his defeat. On July 15th, he announced to the Assembly that he had ordered his troops to leave Versailles, and had recalled Minister Necker. He also recognized Bailly as Mayor of the new government, the Commune of Paris, and Lafayette as Commander of the National Guard. Everyone believed the King to be sincere in his approval of a constitutional form of government.

News of the fall of the Bastille quickly traveled over the country. Soon other cities—Bordeaux, Marseilles, Nîmes, Tours—followed the example of Paris and set up new municipal governments, ousting the old administrations.

Similarly, local divisions of the National Guard were organized. The citizen soldiers took the oath of loyalty to the nation, not to the King, and swore never to take up arms against the people except on orders from the civil authorities.

The rioting of the peasants in the countryside forced the National Assembly to act. The nobles and the clergy, inspired partly by fear and partly by the realization that they were already lost, relinquished their privileges. The old feudal regime was abolished. All duties pertaining to personal servitude were annulled. The Assembly continued to recognize certain other feudal obligations, but these could be redeemed at a price to be determined by that body. On August 11th, tithes to the church were also canceled.

On August 26, 1789, the Assembly proclaimed the Declaration of the Rights of Man and the Citizen, based on the principles stated by the *philosophes* and the concrete demands included in the lists of grievances.

Among the Rights included in the Declaration were:

> "Men are born and remain free and equal in rights."
>
> "The rights of man are liberty, property, security, and resistance to oppression."
>
> "Law is the expression of the general will. Every citizen has a right to participate personally, or through his representative, in its formation. It must be the same for all."
>
> "No person shall be accused, arrested, or imprisoned except in the cases and according to the forms prescribed by law."

> "Since private property is an inviolable and sacred right, no one shall be deprived thereof except where public necessity, legally determined, shall clearly demand it, and then only on condition that the owner shall have been previously and equitably indemnified."

Religious toleration, freedom of speech, and liberty of the press were also affirmed. The national finances were to be controlled by the people, and to them all officials of the state were declared responsible. This was a charter of universal human rights, recognizing neither national boundaries nor distinctions of race nor creed. It was received with enthusiasm by oppressed people everywhere, and was acclaimed particularly in the young United States of America which not long before had itself overthrown British rule on almost the same grounds. In fact, the Rights of Man owed a great deal to the Declaration of Rights of the State of Virginia, as did the American Bill of Rights.

The Constitution awarded the executive power to "a king of the French," to be exercised by responsible agents. The legislative power was vested in a single chamber of 745 members chosen by electors according to a property qualification. But France was not happy under its new constitutional monarchy. The aristocratic members of the Church were resentful of the suppression of religious orders, the confiscation of their properties (1789), and the loss of their revenues, as were most of the nobles who had lost their land. The interruption of trade by the Revolution, together with the sharp decline in spending by the formerly extravagant Court, brought increased unemployment to city workers. The cost of living rose sky-high as speculators bought up the necessities of life, especially grain. The peasants had their own complaints for, while they were nominally free from bondage, they continued to be land-hungry because of the delays in selling property confiscated from the Crown and the emigrés. Only taxpayers could vote; only property owners could be elected to office and were eligible for service in the National Guard. The ordinary workingman was an inactive citizen.

These conflicts soon found expression in different political parties with sharply differing policies. The wealthy section of the Third Estate thought the Constituent Assembly was going too far; the workers of the cities and the peasants believed it was not going far enough. These two main currents of thought were represented, respectively, by the Girondins and the Jacobins.

The Girondins, so-called because most of their leaders came from the Gironde district of Paris, were the moderate republicans. The Jacobins, who took their name from the Jacobin Convent where they held their early meetings, represented the *sans-culottes* (without breeches), the laborers who wore workaday clothes instead of the traditional knee-length breeches (*culottes*) of the upper classes.

Complaints about the Tax-Farm and the manner in which its funds were administered became so bitter that the hated institution had to go. On March 20, 1791, soon after the abolition of the salt tax, the Farm was suppressed. The Farmers-General had been denounced as robbers of the public. It was inevitable that they would be slated for the people's vengeance.

Three months later, Louis XVI was persuaded by one of his generals, in command of emigré forces at Metz, to flee from Paris to join the troops and conduct his own military campaign, without foreign aid. On the night of June 20th, in disguise, he and his family escaped from the Tuilleries. But his carriage was halted at Varennes, where he was recognized, and the King was brought back to Paris under guard. To the people, Louis' flight was outright treason. They called for his deposition and the establishment of a republic.

At this decisive moment, the mass signing of a petition calling for a republic alarmed and frightened the Court and the Constitutionalists. They ordered Lafayette, Commander of the National Guard, to disperse the petitioners; he did so with a volley of musketry. For the first time the more revolutionary faction found themselves in direct collision with the Constitutionalists, and henceforth the battle could not be one of words only.

On April 20, 1792, France declared war on Austria. The Queen and her friends had secretly encouraged an Austrian invasion, while publicly urging the French to sacrifice everything for victory. Under the stress of war, they hoped to insure the continuation of the monarchy. The King believed that a victorious war would aid his cause.

The Girondists, who held the balance of power in the Assembly, hoped to strengthen their party by waging a victorious war in which the dissatisfied people would forget their problems at home. Traditionally, the Girondists had been opposed to Austria and to Louis' marriage to the Hapsburg princess. Now they saw in Austria the threat of returning feudalism and, with it, the loss of their own power.

Most of the nobility, of course, were in sympathy with the enemy; some of them, officers in the French army, were treacherously surrendering to the Austrians whenever the opportunity occurred. The speculators saw a chance to make more money by cornering military supplies and selling them to the army at inflated prices.

But there was another group—those without wealth or influence. New leaders emerging from their ranks denounced the war. Representing the Jacobin Party in the Assembly, these men came to be known as the "radicals." They stood firmly for a republic and bitterly opposed the war, insisting that the chief enemy of the people was at home.

After the French army had met severe defeats, it was recognized that victory was impossible as long as the King and his Court were at the head of the government. The Girondists joined the Jacobins in the demand for a republic. In August 1792, the Assembly suspended the King and ordered elections for a new body, the National Convention, to be elected by universal suffrage. The Commune of Paris assumed police powers in the city, and control of the militia. Leaders in the Assembly appealed to the country to unite and drive out the invaders.

When the Austrian army crossed the frontier, the Paris Commune called on all able-bodied citizens for the national defense. The volunteers were to meet at the Champ-de-Mars, to form battalions and march to the front. With the prisons full of royalists, the soldiers feared for the lives of the families they were to leave behind. These fears, aggravated by tense excitement in the capital, burst into four days of violence. All prisoners in the city jails suspected of royalist sympathies were killed. More than 1,100 were executed during this period known as the September Massacres.

The Prussian army was marching on Paris; its officers were confident of victory because the emigrés had assured them that France was waiting for their arrival. However, the French army of ragged, hastily trained recruits repulsed the Prussians at Valmy on September 20th. Was the key to this victory the determination of an armed people to defend their country, or was it the accuracy of the French gunners and the intensity of their fire, made possible by Lavoisier's improvements in the quality of gunpowder—or both? No one can say. But the Prussians were forced to withdraw, and three months later Lavoisier wrote to the Minister: "The powder mills and magazines of the realm are well supplied; the department is operating at its greatest capacity . . . to enable France to wage the most formidable war."

The victory of Valmy demonstrated that the conquest of Paris would be no picnic.

On September 21st, at its first meeting after the elections, the National Convention proclaimed France a republic. In December, the King was tried by the Convention, sitting as a court, and on January 15, 1793, he was found "guilty of conspiracy against public liberty and of attacks on the general security of the State." The penalty was death.

Up to the last moment, the monarchists tried to prevent the carrying out of the sentence, resorting to demonstrations and even assassination of some of the deputies to the Convention who had voted for it. But their protests were in vain. On Sunday morning, January 21st, to the beating of drums and shouts of "Vive la Nation!" the King was beheaded.

The execution of Louis XVI provoked royalist insurrections in the provinces, and resulted in England's joining the war. Though the Convention vigorously undertook the war, it was torn by struggles between the Girondists and Jacobins. In June 1793, the Girondists were crushed, largely through the efforts of two of the radical leaders, Marat and Robespierre. A republican constitution was adopted but did not go into operation. The government operated by decree through the hastily established Committee of Public Safety, the Committee of General Security, and other agencies such as the Revolutionary Tribunal.

The Reign of Terror began. Thousands of royalists, Girondists, and mere suspects died on the guillotine, under the Convention Law of Suspects. Finally, Robespierre himself, after a brief one-man rule, during which he vainly tried to put into practice the liberal theories of Rousseau, was sent to the guillotine (July 27, 1794) at the direction of the Convention which was frightened by the excesses of the Terror. A period of reaction set in with the death of Robespierre and the ending of the Reign of Terror.

The new Constitution of 1795 was set up by the Directory which governed for the next four years.

Though it seemed to have failed in 1795, the French Revolution had widespread and lasting effects. The bourgeois class was established as the dominant power in France; feudalism was dead. Eventually, political liberty, social equality, and fraternity became the enduring watchwords of a republican France.

# 17. CITIZEN LAVOISIER

*Was Antoine Lavoisier* on the side of the King or the people during the titanic upheaval of the French Revolution? To say that he was wholly for either would not fit the known facts of history. Yet neither can it be said that he stood mutely on the sidelines. The record—his writings, his work, his statements, his acts—tell the tragic story.

In the spring of 1789, when the municipalities were electing representatives who, in turn, were to elect delegates to the Provincial Assembly, Lavoisier had this to say: "Today the nation is too enlightened not to know that its duty is to act in the interests of the majority, that if exceptions are to be allowed in favor of any class of citizens, particularly with regard to taxes, they can be made only in favor of the poor, and that inequality of taxation cannot be tolerated except at the expense of the rich."

But on the question of who should vote for the electors (representatives), Lavoisier was in favor of qualifications based on the ownership of property. Like Turgot, the liberal Minister of Finance appointed in 1774 by the King, he believed that only those who owned land or wealth-producing property should have the right to vote.

As to the character of the national government, Lavoisier was in favor of a constitutional monarchy, patterned on the English system. He thought that the power to make laws should be shared by the King and the people's representatives. The legislative body would rule on taxation and make or change the laws governing trade and internal government. The King would have the power to approve and enforce the laws, and to punish those who broke them. Lavoisier firmly believed, as did many noblemen—Lafayette, Condorcet, Mirabeau, de la Rochefoucauld—that the trouble was not so much with the King as with his advisers. If the King would renounce them and accept a constitution written by the Assembly, which at this time represented mainly the needs of the Third Estate, order could be restored to the country.

Lavoisier had proposed many reforms relating to taxation, agriculture, government finances, education, the rights of the people, and the protection of the citizenry against injustices. He was in favor of uniform taxation with no exemptions for the upper classes, free trade unhampered by provincial border barriers, and uniform systems of currency and weights and measures. He wanted subsidies to expand agriculture for the peasants, abolition of their forced labor (*corvée*) in the service of the nobles and the King, longer leases, and lower interest rates on loans. He proposed a national system of schools with the right to education for everyone. In the field of civil rights, Lavoisier pressed for an end to arrest by *lettres de cachet*, and for the right to a speedy trial before a court of justice. He maintained that individual liberty and freedom of the press in political matters were the "first and most sacred rights" of the people.

He also urged strict control of public funds: there should be a detailed yearly accounting of governmental expenditures, with an annual report to the Assembly. For the priests, who lived in poverty, he recommended larger allowances for living expenses.

With such noted intellectuals as Du Pont de Nemours, Talleyrand, and Condorcet, Lavoisier belonged to two of the many political organizations of the time: the *Club de 1789* and *La Société des Amis Noirs* (Society of Friends of the Black People). The clubs met regularly, the members aired their views, and recommended certain measures they wanted made into laws. The *Société*, organized for the main purpose of ending the flourishing slave trade, worked actively for the freeing of slaves in the French colonies. The *Club of 1789* had among its members not only philosophers and Academicians but the country's richest financiers, all of whom favored the adoption of the Constitution.

Despite its liberal views, the club failed to outlast the year 1789, from which it took its name. The people of Paris looked with suspicion on these rich men who met in fine houses and enjoyed sumptuous dinners after their meetings. The rumor soon spread that the club was financed by Court funds, and the hostility of the people forced its dissolution. By 1791 former members were under suspicion of being traitors to the Revolution. At the same time, the club was despised by the nobles of the Court, who saw it as a threat to royal power. Lavoisier, of course, was caught in the middle, attacked by both sides, at a time when France was in a revolutionary turmoil.

In September 1789, he was elected to the Paris Commune, the new municipal government, from the district of Culture-St.-Catherine. When the National Guard was formed, he was enrolled in the section in charge of the Arsenal, and was still on active duty as late as the autumn of 1793. As Governor of the Discount Bank, he made a financial report to the National Assembly on July 20, 1789, and was commended for his patriotism in keeping up the payments of the Bank, even at the expense of its members' private funds, including his own. He also served on the Gunpowder Commission.

As early as 1790, Lavoisier apparently was uneasy about the outcome of the Revolution. Writing to Benjamin Franklin on February 5th of that year, he remarked:

> "It would be well to give you news of our Revolution; we look upon it as over, and well and irrevocably completed; but there is still an aristocratic party, making some useless resistance and very weak. The democratic party is in the majority and is supported moreover by the educated, the philosophic, and the enlightened members of the nation. Moderate-minded people, who have kept cool heads during the general excitement, think that events have carried us too

far, that it is unfortunate that we have been compelled to arm the people and to put weapons in the hands of every citizen. . . . We greatly regret your absence from France at this time; you would have been our guide and you would have marked out for us the limits beyond which we ought not to go."

In a letter to Joseph Black, dated July 5, 1790, Lavoisier wrote:

"The state of public affairs in France during the last twelve months has temporarily retarded the progress of science and distracted scientists from the work that is most precious to them; but we must hope that tranquillity and prosperity will follow the troubles through which we have passed and which are inseparable from a great revolution."

These words, perhaps better than any, express the concern he felt for the fate of his lifework as a scientist, which he believed to be threatened by the demands put upon him. Many were the state duties he was now called on to perform. His advice was sought by the Committee on *Assignats*, the new paper money (based on the confiscated lands instead of gold) soon to be issued by the National Assembly. The Committee on Taxes needed his help to prepare uniform import duties; he was summoned to find a way to prevent guns from rusting. He was also a member of the Bureau of Consultation of Arts and Crafts, set up to advise the government on inventions and education. And he was still conducting experiments on respiration and oxidation in the body.

For the first time Lavoisier found these continuous demands burdensome. When he was appointed as one of six commissioners responsible for dispensing the funds of the National Treasury, he begged off. Later he accepted, temporarily, but in a letter to the Minister of Public Revenues, he requested that he be allowed to carry out his new duties without pay. "The emoluments that I enjoy as Commissioner for Gunpowder, for the very reason that they are modest, suit my way of life, my tastes, my needs, and at a time when so many good citizens are losing their positions, I could not under any circumstances agree to accept a double salary," he wrote. Of the two posts, he preferred to retain the one that permitted him to work in the Arsenal where for fifteen years he had made his home, and where he had built and equipped his excellent laboratory, largely at his own expense.

The burden of his work and the charges now being leveled against all organizations established by the King during the old regime made Lavoisier eager to give up his offices and limit himself to unpaid tasks. He was considering, perhaps not seriously, taking a vacation and traveling outside of France. In another letter to Black, he wrote on July 24, 1790: "The Revolution that is taking place in France must naturally make some of those attached to the former administration superfluous and it is possible that I may enjoy more freedom; the first use that I shall make of it will be to travel, and especially to travel to England and to Edinburgh to see you."

The hoped-for personal freedom never came, and his

life continued unceasingly to be a busy one. The events of the Revolution made his scientific work more difficult, but at the same time they were favorable to him in other respects.

In 1789, the year of the publication of his *Traité*, Lavoisier was active in the organization of a new journal of chemistry. For some time the authors of the new system of chemical symbols had gone begging for a place to publish. Rozier's *Observations sur la Physique* (Observations on Physics), a monthly journal, was edited by a phlogistonist who was opposed to the new chemistry, while the official publication of the Academy, the only other organ available, had such a backlog of articles that bringing them up to date was hopeless. A new journal was sorely needed.

It was now decided to issue the publication, and Lavoisier helped to organize it. The first issue of the *Annales de Chimie* (Annals of Chemistry) appeared in April 1789, under the joint editorship of Lavoisier, de Morveau, Monge, Berthollet, Fourcroy, de Dietrich, Hasenfratz, and Adet (the last two being the actual authors of the new symbols). The *Annales*, still published today, is the oldest chemical journal in existence. During the many years it has served the science, some of the world's most famous chemists have contributed to its pages.

Apart from his work on human physiology, Lavoisier's main contribution during the next four years was the establishment of a uniform system of weights and measures. France, perhaps more than any other country, suffered from the confusion arising from a wide variety of standards, different areas having different units. When the provincial assemblies drew up their lists of grievances, the Province of Blois recommended this needed reform. As a result, in 1790 the National Assembly requested the Academy of Sciences to formulate a system that could become the basis for measurement not only in France, but in all other nations. (Eventually it became the metric or decimal system, universally used in science today.) The Assembly also voted the sum of 300,000 livres for instruments and other expenses.

As usual, the Academy proceeded to appoint a commission, with various committees to do the necessary work. It included the mathematicians Lagrange and Laplace, Monge, Condorcet, and Lavoisier who was secretary-treasurer. Their completed report proposed the *meter* as the unit of measurement of length. This unit was based on *one fourth* the length of the circle passing around the earth (from the pole to the equator); a meter was to be one $\frac{1}{10{,}000{,}000}$ of this length. A *kilometer* then becomes 1,000 meters, a *millimeter* $\frac{1}{1000}$ meter, and a *centimeter* $\frac{1}{100}$ meter:

| | | | | |
|---|---|---|---|---|
| Meter | (as measured above) | | = | 39.37 inches |
| Centimeter | 0.01 | meter | = | 0.3937 inches |
| Millimeter | 0.001 | meter | = | 0.03937 inches |
| Kilometer | 1,000 | meters | = | 3,280.8 feet |

The committee on which Lavoisier worked was charged with establishing a standard system of weights. This they did by measuring the weight of different volumes of distilled water in a vacuum at 4° Centigrade. The unit they decided upon was the *gram*, which is the weight of distilled water occupying the space of a cubic centimeter. Thus:

| | | | | |
|---|---|---|---|---|
| Kilogram | = | 1,000 grams | = | 2.2 pounds |
| Gram | = | 0.001 kilogram | = | 0.0352 ounces |
| Milligram | = | 0.001 gram | | |

Today while other units (ounces, pounds, and tons; inches, feet, and miles) are still in use, they are generally translated into the decimal system for comparison and for convenience. The metric system was indeed a major contribution growing out of the political revolution in France, and one more in which Lavoisier played a major role.

Late in 1792, when the Academicians made their preliminary report to the National Convention, they referred to it as "a project, which redounds to the glory of the nation and which is useful to all mankind and capable of becoming a new link of universal brotherhood among all peoples who adopt it." In reply, the President of the Convention stated: "Citizens, the National Convention commends the importance and the success of your work. . . . It is through you, worthy men of science, that the world will owe this gift to France."

During the troubled year of 1793, Lavoisier was working on a program for national education he had undertaken at the request of the Bureau of Consultation of Arts and Crafts, of which he had become a member two years earlier. His plan was presented to the National Convention in August of that year, but was published without the author's name.

Lavoisier's educational program advocated a free primary education for all children, as "a duty that society owes to the child." The primary school curriculum should include reading, writing, arithmetic, the elements of natural history and geometry, together with some manual training. He even considered the problem of classroom discipline: pupils might be punished by the teacher, but only after a jury of their fellow students had decided they deserved punishment.

Secondary education would be of two kinds: one course of study for those who would best be served by academic training, in twelve national *lycées*, or high schools, and another for young people who would later engage in mechanical work. Lavoisier's recommendations stressed the second; he was, unknowingly, anticipating the technical education of our century. His report also emphasized the desirability of the interchange of ideas among scientists in different fields. Above all, it underscored the importance to the nation of well-educated citizens:

> "Citizen representatives! The fate of the French republic is in your hands. It rests only with you to raise France to a degree of splendor and prosperity higher than that of any nation . . . Organize education everywhere; give impetus to the useful arts, the sciences, industry, commerce. See with what vigor all other nations, our rivals, are busying themselves with supplying by industry what they lack in power, population, territorial wealth. A nation that does not take part in this general movement, a nation in which the sciences and useful arts languish will soon be outdistanced by rival nations . . . it will finally become the prey of those who decide to invade it . . . Legislators, education made the

Revolution; let education still be your palladium of liberty!"

Lavoisier continued to attend the meetings of the Bureau of Consultation. He was appointed as its President on October 26, 1793.

The suppression of the Academy of Sciences is often cited, by those not in sympathy with the French Revolution, to show that the revolutionists were not interested in, in fact were opposed to, the advancement of science. Similarly, a leading revolutionist (never identified) was said to have declaimed at Lavoisier's trial in 1794: "The Republic has no need of scientists. Let justice take its course!" More than a hundred years later, after carefully sifting the facts, a prominent historian found no evidence of this statement. He called it a legend.

Whatever reasons, right or wrong, the Convention may have had for its decree, it did not abolish the Academy of Sciences out of ignorance. History shows that the Convention fully recognized the importance of science in serving the needs of the people. The reorganization of the *Jardin du Roi* (the King's Garden), and the creation of the National Museum of Natural History (with none of the former inequalities and no royal officers) are but two examples of this. No longer was the museum mainly a promenade for the idle, and the garden only an agreeable meeting place for the nobles. Now able botanists and naturalists worked there, preparing collections and natural history exhibits for the central, or public schools (which, incidentally, were also established at this time).

The Bureau of Longitudes, the *Bibliothèque National* (National Library), the *Ecole Normale Supérieure* (a kind of junior college), and several new medical schools attest to the recognition by the Republic that it needed scholars. At the same time, even friends of the Revolution admit that the suppression of the Academy at that time was a loss to science.

So far-reaching were the effects of the Revolution that it left its mark on the thinking of the people, their art and science, and indeed on every phase of French life. In the Academy of Sciences and the Academy of Art, smaller but just as violent internal revolutions were taking place. The academies originally had been established by the King on a system of rank and privilege. Accordingly, their presidents were nominated by the King from among the honorary members, who were not elected by the other Academicians. New appointments had to be approved by the King after nomination by the elders in the particular science. Only a portion of the Academy had voting privileges, and the position of the assistants as the lowest ranking members was symbolized by their seating arrangement—on benches instead of chairs.

Lavoisier had not been happy with this feudal system of privileged and second-class citizens in a society of equals, and sought to extend voting rights and other powers to all members of the Academy. He also tried, unsuccessfully, to have the members choose their own officers. In 1785, when he was himself appointed Director of the Academy, he asked that the members, rather than the Minister, choose him for presentation to the King.

As Director he succeeded in abolishing the title of "assistant." He urged that membership be extended to three additional categories—physics, natural history, and agriculture. But his proposals were not carried out in the way he wanted. The first two were added for representation on an equal basis with the other sciences, but in agriculture only eight associates were added. He was also unable to secure the vote for the associates, so that inequalities, and of course dissatisfactions, persisted.

There were, in addition, serious financial troubles. The salaries of the Academicians were in arrears. And how were the various projects to be financed out of the depleted national treasury? Of the 300,000 livres voted for the weights and measures project, only 100,000 had been paid by 1791. While pleading for money which was not forthcoming, either for this or for other work of the Academy, Lavoisier himself made personal loans to one or another Academician. But not all of the members showed the same devotion; in fact, some even deserted the society.

Among the latter were nobles, particularly honorary members who had obtained their posts through court favor. These now became emigrés, crossing the frontier or otherwise abandoning their positions. At one meeting Fourcroy demanded that the Academy follow the example of the Royal Society of Medicine, and cross off the membership list all those who had become emigrés, or in other ways had shown their *incivisme*, or opposition to the Revolution.

Similar proposals were being made and acted on in the Royal Academy of Painting and Sculpture, which also had been organized on the model of the old regime.

Jacques-Louis David, the famous painter under whom Madame Lavoisier had studied as a young girl and who had painted the portrait of the Lavoisiers in 1788, was the spokesman for the younger and more revolutionary artists. He firmly believed that to free culture from the shackles of the monarchy, the old system had to be abolished before the new could develop. In all the learned societies the same conflict went on.

While Fourcroy insisted that patriotism required a weeding out of the Academy of Sciences' ranks, others argued that the only business before the organization should be the pursuit of science: it should have no control over the political views of its members. Fourcroy's resolution was defeated. The Academy went on with its meetings, though now they were less well attended.

Though its attendance was reduced and its funds limited, the work of the Academy continued. Lavoisier persisted in his staunch efforts to save the organization to which he had devoted twenty-five years of his life. In a letter to the Committee on Public Instruction he wrote: ". . . time presses; many of the Academicians suffer; several have already left Paris because their means no longer allow them to live there; science, if no one comes to the rescue, will fall into a state of decay from which recovery will be difficult."

The Academy still had a few friends in the Convention and on the Committee of Public Instruction. They argued for the Academy's exemption from the resolution abolishing the learned societies, inserting a clause which stated: "The Academy of Sciences remains provisionally charged with the various tasks entrusted to it by the National Convention . . . Citizens are entitled to combine in free societies to contribute to the progress of human knowledge."

But the exemption clause was lost. David, the painter, gave it the death blow in his speech to the Convention: "In the name of justice, for love of art, and above all for our love of youth, let us destroy, let us annihilate these baneful academies, which cannot exist under a free government." The decree, abolishing all academies and putting their property in the custody of the State, was passed on August 8, 1793.

One of the many projects thus condemned by the decree to remain unfinished business was the work on weights and measures. Balances, standards, and other needed instruments had been ordered for the work, but no provision had been made for their payment or use. Lavoisier tried desperately to have the work continue. He wrote to a member of the Committee of Public Instruction: "I am in need, citizen, of immediate authorizations for these different objects, the more so as the funds that remain in my hands are quite insufficient to supply the needs of Citizens Delambre and Méchain [the astronomers who measured the distance on the earth's surface on which the meter was based]. If the Committee of Public Instruction does not obtain an immediate decision from the Convention on these different points, the work on the weights and measures will be completely suspended." His over-all suggestion was in keeping with the original proposal—to set up a "free society for the advancement of science."

For a time it seemed as though the Academy would be saved. Within a week a new decree was issued, providing for the continuance of the work by the scientists, and for the payment of the annual sums they had received as members. But a few days later the scientists found that their rooms in the Louvre had been placed under seal, forbidding them entrance.

However, a temporary commission was set up, under the leadership of Fourcroy, with the one purpose of completing the work on weights and measures. Ironically enough, Lavoisier was entrusted with the position of secretary-treasurer of this new body, and with his usual industry and devotion he plunged into the project with Laplace, Lagrange, Coulomb, Delambre, and others of his colleagues. But before long his work was again to be interrupted.

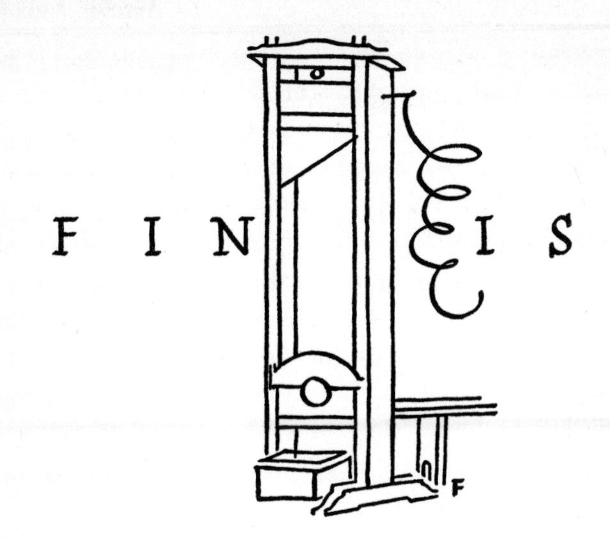


## 18. THE REIGN OF TERROR

*The execution* of the King and the rapid triumphs of the Revolutionary armies frightened Europe's monarchs —most of all King George III of England. His minister, William Pitt, took the lead in organizing the opposition against the French Republic. Spain, governed by a Bourbon king whose family was related to Louis XVI, was easily brought into the war against France. This opened up the Mediterranean Sea to the English, and encouraged the Italian states of Naples and Sardinia to join in the conflict. On all sides the young republic was surrounded by enemy armies: Dutch, Austrian, Prussian, Spanish, and English.

The French armies were inadequate to cover all these fronts, and soon met with reverses. These defeats, with the continued threats of foreign armies, made France's internal enemies more confident. In the western provinces, peasant rebellions were organized by the nobles, and in Lyons and Orléans unemployed workers rioted against the government. Things went from bad to worse. Unemployment increased, and food and other supplies became scarce. Prices skyrocketed as speculators exported grain to dealers in England, who later sold it back to the French at prices far beyond the reach of the poor.

This led to bread riots in Paris and other cities, the hungry people looting stores for food. And when the Convention passed a decree to recruit 300,000 more soldiers, the peasants in the west of France refused to fight, instead organizing themselves into an opposing force, *La Grand Armée Catholique Royale.* There were similar uprisings in the northern province of Brittany, the rebels blaming "false patriots"—the name they gave to the Girondins—for the deplorable conditions. It became clear that the now unpopular Girondins could not wage a successful war on the foreign enemies and at the same time control the dissension within.

The Jacobin opposition in the Convention became strong enough in the spring of 1793 to pass emergency measures giving unlimited power to their representatives, whom they sent out to the districts, cities, and armies. All foreigners were closely watched, and the death penalty was decreed for returning emigrés. A strict censorship of counterrevolutionary writings was set up, confiscation of the property of emigrés and rebels was intensified, and a special tax was imposed on the rich to provide food for the poor. Finally the Jacobins organized the Committee of Public Safety, from which the Girondins were completely excluded.

The Jacobins now were in charge of suppressing rebellions at home and pursuing the war on the national frontiers. But the Girondins did not give up without a struggle. Just before they lost their leadership of the Convention, they arrested and impeached Marat, popularly called the "Friend of the People." Escaping, he went into hiding until his case came before the Revolutionary court, which acquitted him and brought him back in triumph.

In retaliation, and hoping to raise an army of their own to take Paris, the Girondins stirred up trouble against the capital in the outlying districts. The Girondin President of the Convention threatened: "If ever . . . the National Assembly [they refused to use the name "Convention"] should be molested [that is, criticized from the floor], I declare to you in the name of all France, Paris will be destroyed. . . . Soon people will be searching the banks of the Seine to see whether Paris has ever existed."

The final outcome of this bitter parliamentary battle—recriminations, disorderly scenes, accusations and counter-accusations—was the arrest by the Convention of the Girondin leaders, and by June 2, 1793, the Jacobins were firmly in the majority.

But the taking over of power by this group, even though it had the support of the people, still failed to bring about a unified Convention. The struggle within the party itself continued to rage. Danton, who had tried to compromise and conciliate the Girondist Party with the Jacobins, lost his leadership and finally his head. Hébert and his adherents went to the guillotine because their attacks on religion angered the peasants.

Marat also died, not by judgment of the Revolutionary tribunal, like Danton and Hébert, but the victim of assassination by a young woman inspired by the Girondists. As the head of the Jacobin Club when the Revolution was in greatest danger, he had organized the defeat of the Girondists and incurred their everlasting hatred. The murder of the sick and persecuted Marat shocked and horrified all of Paris, for he was considered one of the Revolution's ablest leaders. Now there remained only Robespierre.

This period of French history is know as "The Terror." It was a time of vilification and vengeance, treachery and murder, hasty trials and executions. But there were those who considered it justified. On October 10, 1793, Robespierre defended the desperate measures taken by the Convention: "Either we shall rule or the tyrants will rule us. . . . All the vices fight for them; the Republic has all the virtues on its side. The virtues are simple, poor, often ignorant, sometimes brutal. They are the heritage of the unhappy, the possession of the people. . . . By virtue of five years of treason, by virtue of feeble precautions, and by virtue of our gullibility, Austria, England, Russia, and Italy have had time to set up, as it were, a secret government in France, a government that competes with the French government. They have their secret committees, their treasuries, their agents, they absorb men from us and appropriate them to themselves."

It was against this violent background that the people vented their wrath on the Tax-Farm and everyone associated with it.

The day that Lavoisier joined the organization of tax collectors, his lot was cast with theirs. In spite of his liberal views, his many reforms, and his lifelong devotion and service to the nation, in the minds of the people he was inseparable from those who had become the wealthiest men in France at the expense of the poor. Even the King was less hated than the Farmers-General.

Early in the Revolution, when all sorts of grievances were being voiced, the clerks who worked for the Farm sent petition after petition to the Assembly, demanding an accounting of their pension fund. When in the fall of 1789, the Farmers-General finally sent a statement of the fund's administration, the dissatisfied clerks answered angrily: "Where can one find more cruel masters! . . . If we could examine the accounts supplied to the government by the Farm, what mysteries unknown to the State would be unfolded! . . . Tremble, you who have sucked the blood of the unfortunate and deceived the most beneficent of kings."

The agitation continued, and after abolishing the salt tax, the Assembly responded to popular demand by suppressing the Tax-Farm on March 20, 1791. Lavoisier thus ceased to be a Farmer-General, but his troubles were not over.

A commission, made up of six former members (not including Lavoisier) and three assistants, was charged with settling the Farm's accounts and ending its affairs once and for all. But nearly two years later, on January 1, 1793 (the date set by the National Assembly when the Farm's assets were to have been sold and its accounts cleared), the job had not yet been completed. Public clamor began anew for the turning over to the government of what were believed to be vast accumulated funds.

At the end of February the Convention appointed a new commission to gather information about the crimes and abuses committed by the Farm since the year 1740. There was widespread suspicion that the Farmers-General were deliberately delaying their report, not only to avoid turning over their funds to the Treasury but to make preparations for selling their properties and turning over the "blood money" to the enemies of the Republic.

On June 5th, a decree was passed to dissolve the commission, seal its records, and confiscate the Tax-Farm's funds. In September, Lavoisier was visited by officials of the local government. His papers were searched, and a seal placed on all except those dealing with the work on weights and measures; Fourcroy accompanied the officials to make sure that these remained available.

Within a few weeks the Committee on Finance issued a new decree removing the seals from the papers of the Tax-Farm, permitting the Farmers-General to complete their records, and setting a new date for completion, April 1, 1794. Meanwhile, in an atmosphere where mere suspicion meant established guilt, there were officials of the Farm, who themselves were ready to accuse anyone in order to save their own skins:

It was inevitable that stern measures would be taken against those accused. On November 24th, warrants were issued for the arrest of the Farmers-General, and on the same day eighteen were taken into custody.

Lavoisier could not be found, but the next day he wrote to the Convention, explaining that he should not be held responsible for the delays in completing the Tax-Farm's records since he had not been a member of the commission charged with that task. Should he continue his work for the Commission of Weights and Measures, he asked, or, though he did not consider himself fitted for it, should he work on the accounts of the Farm? His letter was read before the Convention on Public Instruction, but he received no reply. On November 28th, he gave himself up and, with his father-in-law, was imprisoned in Port-Libre with the other Farmers-General.

Characteristically, even under detention, Lavoisier continued with his work. He wrote to his wife, saying that he was making his room more comfortable. "I have begun," he told her, "to adopt a way of life fitted to the circumstances in which I am placed. I worked for two hours and a half yesterday afternoon." He was preparing his *Memoirs on Chemistry,* which he planned to publish in eight volumes. At the time of his arrest, two volumes were ready for the printer, and he was reading the first proofs in prison. He advised Marie not to spend her strength in trying to secure his release.

However, Madame Lavoisier was calling on a number of people in an effort to secure the freedom of her husband and her father. During the month of December, Antoine wrote to her:

> "You give yourself, my dear, much trouble and fatigue of body and mind, and I cannot share it. Take care that you do not injure your health, for that would be the worst of evils. My life is advanced; I have enjoyed a happy existence as long as I can remember, and you have always contributed to it by the devotion that you have shown me. I will leave after me pleasant recollections. My task is done, but you have a right to hope for

a long life, so do not throw it away. I thought yesterday that you were sad. Why be so, since I am resigned to all and look upon all that I shall not lose as gained? Besides, we are not without hope of being together again and, while waiting, your visits give me some happy moments."

The Farmers-General argued, logically, that they could not complete their work in prison without access to their records. Accordingly, they were moved to their former offices, under guard. There conditions were actually worse than at the Porte-Libre prison. Some of the men had no beds; they all suffered from the cold of winter, and lived on what food they could pay for, since none was supplied. They worked at fever pitch, ten hours daily, to complete their accounts, in the vain hope that they would be released when their report was ready. On January 27, 1794, the report was sent to the Committee of Finance. But their release never came.

Meanwhile all their property had been confiscated and their homes were sealed. The final report showed 130,000,000 livres to be owed by the Tax-Farm to the government; this was approximately one-third of the amount they had been accused of withholding from the public. Now new charges were made against the Farmers-General: the adulteration of tobacco, delays in making payments to the Treasury, the collection of excessive rates of interest.

Though Lavoisier had requested that his friends should not take the risk of coming to his defense, a committee from the Bureau of Consultation of Arts and Crafts, headed by Lagrange, his former fellow Academician, submitted a resolution as a "testimony of this esteem" in which Citizen Lavoisier was held. Lavoisier drew up a short account of his career and two more Academicians appealed in his behalf.

The indictment of the Farmers-General was submitted to the Convention on Monday, May 5th, and it was agreed that they should be arraigned before the Revolutionary Tribunal. An observer hurried to the office of the Farmers. Lavoisier was the first person he encountered, and to him he gave the grim news. The worst fears of the Farmers-General were now realized, for the Revolutionary Tribunal was organized to try cases of *incivisme* —counterrevolutionary activity—the one political offense carrying the death penalty.

Some of the Farmers-General had hidden opium in their clothing and now they considered taking their lives, to avoid death on the guillotine. An interesting account of that night was later given by a witness who escaped the mass execution, a young man from the office of the Controller General, who had been detained in the Farmers' offices and expected to share their fate; he, too, was considering suicide. It was suggested to Lavoisier that he end his life with the others.

"Why go to meet death?" he asked them. "Because it is dishonorable to receive it by the decree of another, especially by an unjust decree? . . . We can all face it with confidence in our private lives and in the judgment that will be passed on them. . . . To take our own lives would be to acquit the madmen who are sending us to death. Let us think of those who have preceded us to the scaffold and at all events leave a good example to those who will follow."

Were Lavoisier's words the expression of a stoic resignation in a hopeless situation? Or were they inspired by the religious faith he had preserved in an age of skepticism? Whatever motivated them, they stated the creed of an upright and courageous man. And he did dissuade his fellow prisoners from suicide.

That night all of the Farmers-General were moved to the Conciergerie where the Queen had been imprisoned before her execution. In the morning they were taken before the Revolutionary Tribunal.

The trial was a mockery. There were only four lawyers for the prisoners, and they had only fifteen minutes to prepare the defense. When Lavoisier was asked if he was guilty of fraud against the people, he replied that when abuses had come to his attention, he had reported them to the Minister of Finance, and that he was in a position to prove his statement from authentic documents.

The Farmers-General were returned to the Conciergerie. It was probably during that night that Lavoisier wrote his last letter of which there is a record. It was to a cousin.

> "I have had a fairly long life, above all, a very happy one, and I think I shall be remembered with some regrets and perhaps leave some reputation behind me. What more could I ask? . . . I shall die in full possession of my faculties, and that is another advantage that I should count among those that I have enjoyed. If I have any distressing thoughts, it is of not having done more for my family; to be unable to give either to them or to you any token of my affection and my gratitude is to be poor indeed.
>
> "So it is true that the practice of every social

virtue, important services to one's country, a life spent advantageously in the advancement of the useful arts and of human knowledge, are not enough to protect a man from . . . dying like a criminal!

"I am writing to you today, because tomorrow perhaps I may no longer be allowed to do so, and because it is a comfort to me in these last moments to think of you and of those who are dear to me. Do not forget that this letter is for all those who are concerned about me. It is probably the last that I shall write to you."

The next day, May 8th, the prisoners were given the indictments against them. At ten o'clock that morning they were taken before the Revolutionary Tribunal. Lavoisier's counsel, appointed for him the preceding day, did not appear, but another took his place. At any rate, the proceedings were a mere formality. The jury hastily and unanimously found the accused guilty. The sentence was pronounced and the condemned men were driven in tumbrels to the Place de la Revolution where the executions were held. The carts made their way along the cobblestoned streets Lavoisier knew so well, past the Louvre where the Academy of Sciences had met. On the opposite bank of the Seine was the Mazarin College where he had begun his studies forty years ago.

The order of the executions was in accordance with the order of the names on the list of the indicted. M. Paulze was the third to be beheaded, and Lavoisier, after witnessing his father-in-law's execution, was the next victim of the guillotine. The bodies of the executed were thrown into unmarked graves in the Parc Monceaux cemetery but, ironically, the legal formalities were observed and death certificates were issued.

As distinguished as any scientist in history, the founder of modern chemistry, an expert in political economy and agricultural reforms, the proponent of a national system of education, and an advocate of individual liberty as the most sacred right of man, Lavoisier was condemned because he was a Farmer-General, a Commissioner for Gunpowder, and a member of the Royal Academy of Sciences. These associations brought about his death and, with it, a tragic and incalculable loss to science.

"Only a moment to cut off that head," said Lagrange, "and another hundred years may not give us another like it."

# BIBLIOGRAPHY


BROWN, M. W.: Painting of the French Revolution. Critics' Group, 1938.

DUVEEN, DENIS I.: L'explication de la mort de Lavoisier. Arch. Internat. d'Hist. d. Sciences, vol. 9, no. 34, 1956.

DUVEEN, DENIS I.: Antoine Laurent Lavoisier and the French Revolution. J. Chem. Education 131:60, 1954.

DUVEEN, DENIS I.: Madame Lavoisier (1758–1836). Chymia. Annual Studies in Hist. of Chemistry, 4:13, 1953.

DUVEEN, DENIS I.: Catalogue of Printed Works by and Memorabilia of Antoine Laurent Lavoisier (1743–1794), exhibited at the Grolier Club, New York, Feb.-Mar., 1952.

DUVEEN, DENIS I., and KLICKSTEIN, H. S.: Benjamin Franklin and Antoine Laurent Lavoisier. Franklin and the New Chemistry. Ann. Science 2:103, 1955.

DUVEEN, DENIS I., and KLICKSTEIN, H. S.: Antoine Laurent Lavoisier's Contribution to Medicine and Public Health. Bull. Hist. Med., 29:164, 1955.

DUVEEN, DENIS I., and KLICKSTEIN, H. S.: Two early American Eulogies on Lavoisier. J. Hist. Med. & Allied Sciences, vol. 8, no. 4, 1953.

FEUCHTWANGER, L.: Proud Destiny. Viking Press, 1947.

FOSTER, MARY LOUISE: Life of Lavoisier. Smith College Monographs, No. 1, 1926.

FRENCH, SIDNEY J.: Torch and Crucible: The Life and Death of Antoine Lavoisier. Princeton Univ. Press, 1941.

GERSHOY, LEO: The French Revolution and Napoleon. F. S. Crofts & Company, 1933.

GIBBS, PHILIP: Men and Women of the French Revolution. J. B. Lippincott, 1906.

GRIMAUX, E.: Lavoisier. Third edition, 1899.

HAYES, CARLTON J. H.: A Political and Social History of Modern Europe. The Macmillan Company, 1928.

HENDERSON, E. F.: Symbol and Satire in the French Revolution. G. P. Putnam's Sons, 1912.

HOLT, ANNE: The Life of Joseph Priestley. Milford, 1931.

JAFFE, BERNARD: Crucibles. The Lives and Achievements of the Great Chemists. Tudor Publishing Company, 1934.

LAVOISIER, A. L.: Correspondence. Annotated by René Eric. Albin Michel, 1955.

LAVOISIER, A. L.: Méthode de Nomenclature chimique proposée par MM. de Morveau, Lavoisier, Bertholet et de Fourcroy, 1787. (English translation by James St. John, "Method of Chemical Nomenclature," 1788.)

LAVOISIER, A. L.: Traité élémentaire de Chimie, 1789. (English translation by Robert Kerr, "Elements of Chemistry," 1790.)

MARTIN, KINGSLEY: The Rise of French Liberal Thought. New York Univ. Press, 1954.

MCKIE, DOUGLAS: Antoine Lavoisier: Scientist, Economist, Social Reformer. Henry Schuman, 1952.

PADOVER, S. K.: A Jefferson Profile as Revealed in His Letters. John Day Company, 1956.

SCHAPIRO, J. SALWYN: Condorcet and the Rise of Liberalism. Harcourt, Brace & Company, 1934.

SMYTHE, DAVID MINDERS: Madame de Pompadour. Wilfred Funk, 1953.

# INDEX